the anatomy of grace

peter w. marty

Augsburg Fortress
MINNEAPOLIS

THE ANATOMY OF GRACE

Cover design: Kevin van der Leek
Book design: Michelle L. N. Cook

Library of Congress Cataloging-in-Publication Data

Marty, Peter W., 1958-
The anatomy of grace / Peter W. Marty.
p. cm.
Includes bibliographical references.
ISBN 978-0-8066-8045-3 (alk. paper)
1. Grace (Theology)--Meditations. 2. Devotional calendars--Lutheran Church. I. Title.

BT761.3.M325 2008
248.4--dc22

2008028040

The paper used in this publication meets the minimum requirements of American National Standard for Information Sciences — Permanence of Paper for Printed Library Materials, ANSI Z329.48-1984.

Manufactured in the U.S.A.

12 11 10 09 08 1 2 3 4 5 6 7 8 9 10

To Susan Ward Marty,

who has given me not only a "W" to center my name,

but countless other graces to center my life

contents

ordinary grace

surprising grace

mysterious grace

weightless grace

Introduction

Freshman biology class was an eye-opener for me. The transition from middle school science where we *talked* astronomy, to high school science where we *handled* amphibian guts, was slightly traumatic. Frog dissection came only five weeks into the school year. With it came the distinct odor of formaldehyde. The smell accompanied me everywhere I went. Even my frog-scented lab pencil made its presence known every time I drew it toward my face while pondering a story problem in math class. Then there was the personal adjustment of wondering why so many frogs had to die for our seemingly inconsequential biology class in Brookfield, Illinois. Where was any justice in this death industry? Every time I started to do the mental arithmetic of how many high schools in America must be engaging in the very same lab experiment, my discomfort grew. Why did a presumably happy frog have to end up splayed, belly-side up, across my dissection pan?

Well, I did what I was supposed to do and what everybody else did. I pinned the limbs of my frog to the tray using the long needles the teacher provided. Alex, the smart aleck across the table, kept hooking electrodes to his frog's hind legs, hoping to create the perfect muscle spasm that would cause his frog to leap. It never quite worked. Eventually, Alex pinned his frog down just like mine, in the same spread-eagle position.

I learned two things of lasting importance from this freshman dissection class. First, medical school was probably not in my future, at least not if surgery or cadaver work were part of the regimen. Fingering slimy organs and spongy tissue didn't exactly appeal to me. But second, I discovered a whole world behind the seen world that I had been accustomed to taking for granted. We all learned the details of what makes life happen for a frog, and later for a fetal pig, and, by extension, a human being. As we put our scalpels, scissors, and forceps to work, we began to understand organ structure and function. We soon became experts at distinguishing sub-systems within the body cavity, all of which functioned interdependently. When I was lucky, my line diagram of these internal systems matched the teacher's outline on the overhead projector. That minor success was a special thrill for a non-science kid.

Similar to my four-legged friend's body in the gray dissection tray, our human body is not just one external entity devoid of internal intricacy. The very viability of our lives depends upon a skeletal system and muscular system that work well. We all possess a nervous system and an endocrine system that play a significant role in our health. And, of course, there are the respiratory, reproductive, and digestive systems. The anatomical relationship between these and other systems, first sketched by Leonardo da Vinci as early as the fifteenth century, remains a part of the hidden wonder in all our bodies.

The science of anatomy aims to reveal that which can be seen with the naked eye and that which cannot. It is basically a study of structure and form. Originally, researchers made all of their discoveries about the internal structure and form of a body through dissection, or the "cutting up" of body tissue and organs. The word *anatomy* comes from the Greek *ana,* meaning "up" or "through," and *tome,* meaning "to cut."

This book aims to look at grace anatomically. That is, it seeks an "up and through" glimpse of the different ways that God reveals what it really means to be a God who consistently acts in our favor. If most people have at least some elemental, if largely unformed, understanding of grace, and I think they do, what would it look like if we could cut and slice that picture of grace more deeply? What would the contours of God's grace look like in our lives, our churches, and our world if we could peer beneath the more common definitions of grace that occupy the surface of so much religious talk?

I must confess that grace is my favorite word in the Christian vocabulary. It rings with a priority of divine generosity, outpacing every other form of gift-giving ever known to the world. Though it defies easy classification, grace is a beautiful word that has a way of intoxicating all who care to load up their hearts with the riches of faith. Sometimes we have to pause long enough, or probe deeply enough, to notice the presence of grace so near to our immediate experience. But we are never without it. It is shorthand for everything that God is willing to do for us in our often tired and tragic but nevertheless blessed lives. Like some great giveaway, grace is the love of God poured out to people who do not deserve it—people who could do nothing to obtain it even if they were determined to have it. Many people inside and outside of the Christian fold know something about these outlines of grace. But what else can we learn about the specific behavior of grace in shaping a life, and the nature of grace in forming a Christian community? Here's where we must turn anatomical.

If our bodies run on a network of elaborate systems, whose functions are linked together to perform a general task, we might say something similar about the underpinnings of grace. Grace has its own distinct channels of operation. The delivery system by which grace comes into contact with our daily lives is not a set of complex organs or intricate systems with specific functions. No, think of grace as taking the form of different *expressions*. There are certain ways one can look for grace to behave and make itself known, even if this behavior is rarely tame. There are particular paths that grace tends to follow as it emerges in our lives. It arrives on the doorstep of our hearts in different forms.

For the purpose of this work, I have identified six expressions for the way grace seems to operate. Call them character traits of grace, if that is helpful. But aim to view these traits not as rigid classifications but supple ones, lest grace be stripped of the very freedom and nonconformity that give it such power.

1. Grace often makes a *serendipitous* appearance in our lives. It seems to show up almost by accident, yet does so often when we need it the most. Like the non-essential yet embellishing grace notes in a musical score, whose beauty is unmistakable, grace carries a similar splendor, possessing an over-the-top quality of unanticipated and even ornamental loveliness.

2. Frequently, grace moves with *unobtrusive* calm, gliding completely under the radar. Not interested in the noise and lights of life, this form of grace comes to us quietly, with no greater purpose than to land us back on our feet when we've lost our way. Sometimes it seems to call out from its obscurity, hoping we might at least notice its presence.

3. *Ordinary* grace is that which dresses up in the clothes of everyday life. Many of our encounters with this kind of grace come through the most common experiences. They are stitched into the garment of routine. These expressions of grace do not seek to be glamorous. If anything, they are most at home in the rough and tumble of life, working through our different fragilities, and adjusting to where we happen to be at a given moment.

4. Wonder-filled grace is the *surprising* variety. This kind of grace is the dazzling antidote to life that has been stripped of wonder and flattened by those who walk all over joy. It is the fresh expression of God that is new every morning, when we wake up into a world that we did not create.

5. Grace that is *mysterious* could not rhyme with common sense if it tried. It neither fits the framework of fairness nor holds up well to the laws of logic. Expressions of grace that appear in this mysterious way defy both measurement and manipulation. They operate according

to the odd principles of divine math, where two plus two equals five.

6. The final expression of grace in this anatomical outline is *weightless*. We know this unencumbered form of grace to appear almost effortlessly. Uninterested in forcing itself upon us, this grace does not take itself too seriously. In fact, it is often marked by levity and humor. If morality lends heaviness to much of life, and legalism drowns the human spirit, the lightness of grace is a precious buoy of hope.

The essays in this volume are reflections on these six anatomical expressions of grace. The collection is both idiosyncratic to my life as a pastor and radio host, yet resonant with the language of the church and the majesty of scripture. One thing the chapters all have in common is their origin. They spring from a heart that is pastorally driven—one that on its best days is tuned to the heartbeat of God and the pulse of grace evident in other people.

I make no claims to some flawless structural model of grace, any more than I intend this to be a comprehensive treatment of the subject of grace. Were grace reducible to fit within neat conceptual boundaries, it would no longer be grace. It might be religion, but it wouldn't be grace.

Readers may want to utilize the fifty-two essays in devotional fashion, one for each week of the year. The book is neither a progressive journey nor a liturgically rhythmed book, making room for one to digest it in morsels. If Philip Yancey is right, that our world is "starved for grace," chewing on the different chapters of this book for several days at a time might inspire creative nourishment in the minds of those who want a fresh take on life.

Much of our experience with the very concept of grace depends upon some play and flexibility with our language. We don't always need religious wording to reveal holy thoughts. In fact, religious talk seldom takes readers or listeners anywhere significant. Too often it turns into theological jargon that has little impact on transforming lives. Jesus embodied grace every day. He championed it like no other individual. But he never used the word—not ever. That conspicuous absence of any mention of grace should be our own cue for thinking as imaginatively as we can about what the Apostle Paul called this "indescribable gift" of God (2 Cor. 9:15). If we can find fresh ways to observe grace at work in our world, without obsessing over the naming of it, chances are good that life will flow with more gratitude than we ever knew possible.

The people of St. Paul Lutheran Church, Davenport, Iowa, the congregation I presently serve, are to me what Paul calls "a letter of Christ . . . written not with ink but with the Spirit of the living God" (2 Cor. 3:3). They possess extraordinary faith and vitality, typically spending more energy giving thanks for life's blessings than counting them. The God-shaped ways they seem to handle joy and sorrow inspire my life in a daily way. A number of the essays here are adaptations of what I shared with these dear saints over a period of years.

To the many listeners of *Grace Matters* radio, I am equally indebted. Were it not for their generous spirit and lively partnership every week of the year, I'm certain that my understanding of grace would be greatly impoverished. My thanks to Don Ottenhoff and the Collegeville Institute for Ecumenical and Cultural Research for such warm hospitality when this book was in its early stages; to Becky Harper, my administrative assistant, for detailed help in the late stages; and to Susan Johnson at Augsburg Fortress, for guiding the entire project so competently. Finally, the editorial savvy in scrutinizing much of my writing, and the keen sense for ministry in colleague Mary Miller, make her not only a trusted friend, but "grace upon grace" in my life as well.

serendipitous grace

serendipitous grace

distinct notes

The dim, crooked piano light casts a warm night's glow on the living room walls. It's almost subject matter for Norman Rockwell. Near the upright piano, a chrome fold-up music stand—the $14.95 variety that a sneeze can upend—lists helplessly to the left. In front of the stand, a ten-year-old girl with pigtails sits on a stool, tilting her head gently to one side. She raises her flute to play, puckers her lips, and then lets a mighty rush of raspy wind sail through the chamber of the flute. This girl is ready to make music. Her arms seem barely long enough to hold the instrument comfortably. But never mind. As far as she is concerned, it's a perfect fit. Her smile says so.

Dad has asked and received permission to listen in on "the concert." He has this confident musician's look about him, even though he is not a musician and has never touched a flute. Rachel's music is no more complicated than "Tea for Two." But it's a major orchestral piece when you're in fourth grade just beginning to read notes. She struggles to get out a detectable pitch. *Sweet* sound would not yet be the description. Both father and daughter erupt in laughter. Her twelve-year-old brother comes in to investigate. He unhelpfully sings along, as if to pretend he is lending crucial musical support.

As you may gather, there are new sounds emanating from the Marty household. It's more than a sight to behold; it's a sound to behold! Adding a new note every other day to one's octave repertoire gets pretty exciting. This obviously can't go on for too long. There's a limit to the range of every flutist. But for the moment, anything and everything seems possible. When Rachel unpacks her flute, pushing the head and foot joints into the body joint, giving them each a professional twist, one would think she is preparing for a symphony audition with a platinum Powell instrument in hand. Even the pretty pink swab cloth appears to have a special sanctity about it. The discovery that one's own lips can actually make music, when positioned over a tiny mouth hole . . . this brings unbounded joy! It's a joy that I can only hope will stay with Rachel, in some small measure, when the tedium of practice soon gets the best of her.

A critical listener might wonder if all of the distorted sounds derived from Rachel overblowing a basic scale is really music. Well, of course it's music. George Ives, the father of the early twentieth-century composer Charles Ives, was a song leader with perfect pitch in his nineteenth-century congregation. In that Danbury, Connecticut, choir was a stonemason by the name of John Bell, a man who always bellowed off key. When someone once asked Ives how he could stand that raucous quality in his choir, he replied: "Old John is a supreme musician. . . . Watch him closely and reverently, look into his face and hear the music of the ages. Don't pay too much attention to the sounds—for, if you do, you may miss the music."[1]

The Apostle Paul, trying to make a point about the gift of speaking with clarity, used a simile about playing the flute: "It is the same way with lifeless instruments that produce sound, such as the flute or the harp. If they do not give distinct notes, how will anyone know what is being played?" (1 Cor. 14:7). Paul obviously didn't have a fourth grader in his house. If he had, he would have known to look closely and reverently right into her face. What I bet he would have seen is all happiness. What I bet he would have heard is glorious music.

the poetry of sheep

Occasionally, a publisher will send a book manuscript my way, asking for a review that might aid some front-end marketing. It happened again last week. I didn't have time to read and review this one, nor did I have great interest in it. In this case, the author had written a treatise on why the church has so thoroughly failed young adults. *Disillusionment* and *disappointment* are favorite words in her argument. The author asks, with more cynicism than innocence, "What does going to church every Sunday really have to do with anything?"

My first response to the book is this: if your expectations in life are unreal, your disappointment will be huge. If in starting a family your expectation is that you will enjoy unceasing harmony, selfless devotion of kids to parents, and a constant romance of support and togetherness—look out! Your fall will be great. If your expectation for church is the thrill of one euphoric experience after another, you'll probably never return. If on the other hand you view the church of Jesus Christ like a verdant garden, you may feast forever. Yes, it's full of sweet corn *and* manure, both holiness *and* holy mess. But it is still the garden of God's grace.

My second response is: church is always about more than satisfying personal desires and hanging around like-minded people. At least it ought to be. It is a community in which we have a realistic shot at being changed, once we've immersed our lives in the joys and sorrows of everyone else's lives. It offers an unsurpassed opportunity to suddenly stop life, at least once a week, and give collective thanks for blessings too many to number.

My third response is: some of the beauty and significance of church is total mystery. Why certain people would bother to love others, forgive others, and serve others in the peculiarly Christlike way they do is beyond comprehension. Metaphorically speaking, it's like a jumble of words coming together to form an unexplainably rich poem. My inspiration for this metaphor comes, of all places, from a sheep farm in northeastern England. A writer there, Valerie Laws, received a public Arts Council grant of £2,000 (roughly $3,600 at the time) to create a living poem with living sheep. She spray-painted a single word onto the back of every sheep. As the sheep wander about, the words take on a new poetic form every time they come to rest. If you've been waiting for an organic kind of haiku poetry, this is it. The only way to read the poetry, in case you're wondering, is from a raised platform.

Something tells me this is a pretty good image for the church. "We are the people of [God's] pasture and the sheep of [God's] hand," says the psalmist (Ps. 95:7). When trying to spell out what this meant one day, Jesus spoke of calling each of his sheep by individual name and leading them. According to the Gospel writer John, this was such a strange figure of speech Jesus was using that the people "did not understand what he was saying to them" (John 10:6).

It would do us well in the church to think of God writing poetry with our lives. You can't write a poem with one word. It takes a whole flock. Half the time, we seem a jumbled mess. Sometimes we fight over our place. Other times, some inept or uninterested hired hand steps in and allows the slightest sign of trouble to scatter the flock. But always, God is trying to figure out how to get us to be this unexplainably rich poem we're capable of being.

On those days when the poem doesn't fall together just right, it may be that some key words are missing. The poem is incomplete without them. Says Jesus, "I have other sheep that do not yet belong to this fold. I must bring them also" (John 10:16). Their inclusion in the flock, we may surmise, would make for the most eloquent and complete of poems.

blaze

Summer weekends in the small city where I live can get *slow*, evidently slow enough to give some young people a real sense of boredom. That's what must have happened one Saturday night last month when two young men decided to break into our church.

It was a blistering hot night. I was sound asleep beneath the noise of the air conditioner's hum. Somehow I missed hearing the phone ring. The police were calling to inform me that a burglary was in process at our church. As it turns out, two students from a respected out-of-town college had entered our building in the middle of the night, unaware that the entire facility is equipped with a silent alarm. The police arrived in a flash and apprehended the two men on the premises. They were taken to the county jail, and each was given a $10,000 bond.

Back at the church the next day, several of us began the process of trying to figure out what would possess two presumably nice young men to burglarize a church. We knew it was a hot night. But did they need air conditioning that badly? Yes, they were intoxicated. The police report said as much. But did they really believe that an AA support group was meeting in St. Paul Lutheran Church at 2:35 in the morning? Of course they were busy convincing each other that they could pull off a heist. But did they really believe they were smarter than a security system? We pondered all of the possibilities. Why did they break in?

The clue to cracking the case appeared on the third page of the police report. Officers on the scene confiscated one item of the church that was in their possession at the time of the arrest. The officer's written description of the stolen property: "A booklet entitled, *BLAZE: God Feeds Us.*" Catch this: two thieves break in and steal a fifth-grade Sunday school book! Imagine the audacity of making off with some little kid's book about God. Of all the things they could have stolen, from a left-behind camp sleeping bag in the lost-and-found pile to a spare bottle of communion wine—either of which would have suited these drunks well—they went for a Sunday school book. Have you ever heard of such spiritually motivated thieves?

My curiosity was up enough to sit down and read *BLAZE*. I started into the twenty-nine pages, hoping for clues to their fascination with the text. It was captivating. I began to picture these guys huddled under the dim beam of an exit light, scrambling to speed read the contents of this little book before the police arrived. Wouldn't that make for a great promotional video by the publisher? The first story in the book, it turns out, gives *BLAZE* its subtitle. Jesus miraculously feeds 5,000 people. The reader is challenged to see all of the ways that God still feeds us. The richness, the grace, the nourishment of God's Word keeps working its own miracles. It's good stuff. This is what our thieves would have read had the police allowed them to finish.

But phooey on those cops. They took the book away. They left these guys alone in their jail cells bereft of any nourishment—nothing to read in the way of inspiration from God. It could be that the arresting officer liked the book so much that he took it home and digested the contents himself. But I doubt it. The estimated value he assigned the precious little book when writing up his police report was a whopping $0.00. Oh, the mysteries of God's Word. To some it's priceless, even worth a night in jail; to others it's cheap, worth little more than a trip to the landfill.

autumn purple ash

Every year in the month of May, great words of advice and inspiration rain down on mortar-boarded heads, trying to unstiffen them for the wonders and worries of the years ahead. Celebrities get overpaid on these days. Some unspectacular people end up delivering the most spectacular truths. But the best commencement speeches seem to address the human spirit in all of its possibility and responsibility.

Here is journalist Elizabeth Drew reaching out to the minds of graduating seniors at Reed College a generation ago. I wasn't there, but reading Drew makes me want to pick up more of her writing:

> If you think about life in terms of what you are going to do, what you are going to accomplish, you're leaving out big parts of it. Don't lose touch with your capacity to see absurdity, to laugh—including at yourselves—to enjoy, to take time out from striving, and just be. Don't lose touch with your capacity to love; in fact, nurture it, for you will find that it is something that can grow. Let yourself need people, and let them need you. Don't forget to take time out to look at the trees. If you do lose those things, you will have lost a great deal. And what are most commonly recognized by the outer world as accomplishments will have a certain emptiness. [2]

Never mind if you are not graduating from any institution in the near future or preparing to frame some diploma for which you worked so hard. There are still marvelous nuggets of insight for you tucked into Drew's words. When is the last time you were able to really laugh at yourself? Can you remember praying for God to help you take time out from striving so hard? How is your capacity for loving these days? My favorite admonition of hers is about the trees: *Don't forget to take time out to look at the trees.*

I've been looking at trees a lot recently, especially the young autumn purple ash in the center of our front yard. I study that silly tree every day and wonder the same sort of things a doctor probably wonders when he looks at me: "How is it going?" I'm thinking it's now time to start talking to this ash tree. "How are you doing today? What does it feel like to be sinking in some roots with our family? Do you like the way Jacob and Rachel are watering you, or are you drowning?" What I don't have the nerve to ask the tree is whether it has had a visit yet from the dreaded emerald ash borer. When I spotted some holes on its leaves a couple weeks ago, I frantically called the man in the little green and white truck. He climbed out with his rubber boots on, green pants tucked into the boots, white button-down shirt tucked into the pants. When I saw the clipboard, I knew we were in for serious diagnostic work.

By the time the truck drove off, it felt like sucking and chewing insects were crawling up my arms. The autumn purple ash, his "complimentary analysis" read, had leafhopper and sawfly bugs. The lilac bush had aphids infesting it. The yew had spider mites. The crabtree had Apple Scab. What on earth is Apple Scab? Worst of all, he hung a little zipper-top plastic bag on the front door with big red lettering on it: *Look what we found!* Inside was a little ash leaf with holes shot through it.

I put the estimate for recommended treatment on the counter for my wife Susan to see. The plastic bag stapled to it added extra drama. When I headed down to my study to begin Monday's writing project, I did what I always do. I gazed out the window, hoping to find inspiration for words and ideas that sometimes come so painstakingly slow. There in the little fruit tree just feet from my window was a hummingbird. I saw that little ornithological wonder, wings moving as if at the speed of light, and I forgot all about leafhopper and sawfly bugs. The words began to flow.

Don't forget to take time out to look at the trees.

lost and found

Every museum, school, and church in the world seems to have a lost-and-found table. I have rifled enough times through our church's own table bearing the same name to know that the "lost-and-found" name is a complete misnomer. Nothing presently on our lost-and-found table has yet to be "found," certainly not by its true owner, and nothing strewn across it may ever be. Every item sits patiently and quietly, week after week, hopelessly separated from its rightful owner. I pored over the contents of our table's treasures, trying to decide what we should do with a pile of goods that no one ever seems interested in reclaiming. At our church, we collect enough misplaced goods in the course of a few months to open a big box store. Virtually everything under the sun has appeared in our handsome collection, with the possible exception of dentures.

The Kansas City Public Library's stash of lost items grew so large that one of the librarians there took it upon herself to begin logging all of the objects found sandwiched in the pages of returned books. Her inventory was fascinating. Everything from a slice of cooked bacon to a flattened silver turtle made the list. She has found two magnetic hotel door keys, one pair of 3-D glasses, one chicken bone, one French fry, one gummy worm on a plastic stick, one St. James Place mortgage card from a Monopoly game, and one Kool brand cigarette. There was even a color photograph of Ex-Lax products.

This librarian's greatest find, however, was a 3 x 5-inch card with five words printed in pencil on it: "Thanks for all you do." Now *that* is a treasure. Maybe it was just a bookmark, accidentally left behind. But equally possible, maybe it wasn't. Perhaps that little card was one library user's gentle appreciation for the poor soul who has to peel a dried French fry off the page of a tender novel, or scrape a flattened turtle from inside a dictionary. Who's to say? I can think of plenty of people doing other thankless work who would love to stumble upon a similar sign of grace, just as modest. The restaurant custodian who picks cigarette butts out of the urinal is one. The utility lineman working the night shift to restore power through the latest ice storm is another.

Thanks for all you do. Words on a lost index card that meet the eyes of a finder—a message of grace in a sometimes grace-less world—precious meaning received in the midst of monotonous routine. How wonderful to feel noticed when we're down on life or lost in a maze of mundane tasks. Hearing a gracious word from another is almost like being found—being rescued. When we get off track and lose sight of meaningful things and important relationships, to be retrieved is the most wonderful feeling in the world. The blessing of having someone find or notice us refuels our hope. We start to regain our bearings.

I think of the Corinthian Christians trying to form a congregation in the midst of a wild culture. Hard drinking and sexual promiscuity were the norm in Corinth. Imagine how encouraging it must have felt to receive a hand-written note from the Apostle Paul far away, especially when the opening line read: "I always thank God for all of you."

The important thing we want to keep in mind is this: Whenever we get lost in some inglorious duties of a given day or find ourselves bereft of meaning because of mindless tasks or unbelievable challenges, we have a Lord who keeps watch. This Lord tends to us in moments when we may feel forsaken, like unclaimed items on a lost-and-found table. Faith tells us that God does not wait for someone else to reclaim us and get us back on our feet. God initiates the reclamation project and pursues us. Every so often we notice this strong behavior of God, and we say: *Thanks for all you do.* Oh, how those five words must gladden the heart of God!

cleaning house

If more than one person lives in your house, chances are good that several competing cleaning styles vie for center stage. One person may believe that every stray bread crumb must be wiped up within its first minute of homelessness, while another soul under the same roof, possibly bearing an identical surname, is content to leave the newspaper strewn across the kitchen table for days, with the idea that some other family member may want to recall what last weekend's weather was.

My household is typical—if typical means *wide variety* in the school of neatness. Never mind who behaves in what fashion. Put the four of us together and you have an amalgamation of tidiness and slobbery cohabiting inside four walls. As a week progresses, one out-of-place item soon becomes two, then four, then eight, then ninety-eight. Messiness grows faster than mold. A lost shoe becomes part of the décor. A dropped hat ends up a toy for the dog. Before long, the slow and quiet accumulation grows to an unbearable level. That's when we don SWAT team gear and sweep the place cleaner than Martha Stewart's own home. It's effective and dumb, all in one. You'd think we would learn a different rhythm one of these years.

The problem we face may be similar to the one you face: stuff accumulates gradually without any particular announcement or fanfare. A mess multiplies unobtrusively. Suddenly a pile exists where there was no pile at all.

It seems that our lives follow a similar path. Our little unbecoming decisions, tiny irritating behaviors, and seemingly inconsequential actions do not appear to accumulate with any adverse effect on our spiritual lives. But they do. They grow slowly. They multiply. Little misdeeds and quiet and unhealthy attitudes cake our lives with layers of unholiness. A little grime of casual error turns into the embedded grease of sin.

In C. S. Lewis's *The Screwtape Letters*, Screwtape is a senior devil advising an apprentice devil, Wormwood, on how best to move Christ out of the center of our lives. He reminds Wormwood that the size of the sin doesn't matter at all. The object is to move us "away from the light and out into the searing cold of nothingness."[3] Contrasting greater sin to lesser sin, Screwtape says: "Murder is no better than bitterness, if bitterness can do the trick. Indeed the safest road away from God is the gradual one. The gentle slope, soft underfoot, without sudden turnings, without great events, without signposts. Suddenly you reach a destination not planned but so easily arrived at."[4]

The safest road away from God is the gradual one. Troubles with our faithfulness mount in incremental ways without tendering much notice. One day we wake up with our life in total chaos and wonder where it all came from.

The beauty of being able to introduce a confessional component into one's faith life is that it opens the door to cleaning house. It gives a breath of daily freshness that can allow for a more focused attack on the grime in our lives. Few things kill the luster in life more effectively than grime accumulating into a greasy build-up. So practice some new spiritual habits and establish some new rhythms for cleaning up your real estate—your physical house, your emotional house, and your spiritual house. Are you up to the task? Of course you are.

chasing butterflies

In a *Peanuts* comic strip, Snoopy sits atop his doghouse as Woodstock whizzes by. Snoopy's little yellow bird friend first flies chaotically to the right in a scrambled pattern. In the next panel, Woodstock flies to the left in the same kind of erratic twisting and turning fashion; a curly and meandering line indicates the bird's flight. Finally exhausted, Woodstock lands on the doghouse. Snoopy, having observed what the chase has been all about, says to his friend, "Never fall in love with a butterfly!"

Woodstock is many things to many people. In the case of this one strip, he's my hero. He does what I don't do well enough: he purses life's affections regardless of how many unpredictable directions that pursuit may require.

Last May, I took part in a ritual many parents observe on late spring weekends—a college graduation ceremony. As I looked out over a sea of graduates, I wondered to myself how many of these mortar-boarded people knew their next move. Which ones really had a clue whether they were going to be selling aluminum siding by telephone or working in a stem cell research lab in suburban Baltimore? Which graduates had the foggiest idea what they would do with their feet when the alarm clock went off the next morning? Pondering the future of those graduates was a mental game of guessing on my part. It didn't last long. I quit.

I quit the game for my own good. Goal orientation is essential in life. But it also has limits. Why, I began to ask myself, are we always hung up with knowing a precise destination? Sure, many human endeavors require that an effort bring certain results. A fullback must eventually get the football across the goal line if he wants to keep his job. A real estate agent would be wise to close on a deal every now and then. A physician ought to have some idea of what she hopes her patient will look like once the restorative surgery is finished. But not everything needs to have a goal. Sometimes the "way" itself is the goal. Relationships are not goal-oriented, or they were never meant to be. Admittedly, there will always be people eager to "conquer" someone of the opposite sex, or curry political favor from another with power, or climb in a career by staying close to a well-placed colleague. But when there is health in our perspective on relationship, we don't decide who we want as friends and then develop an action plan to achieve our goal. No, we share good times, delicate communication, and deep meaning with those whom we care to be around. The process of experiencing all of this is itself the goal.

Life is a journey. What makes this journey an adventure is that we don't always know the destination. The delightful word for this experience is *serendipity*. Serendipitous living means that we will make surprise discoveries while on a journey somewhere else. If everything in our lives had to have a goal with measurable results, we would never know the good pleasure of serendipity. Pity that condition! I'm telling you, it's not how you want to live. Every day deserves to have some degree of serendipity creeping into your otherwise predictable life.

Faith is its own serendipitous journey. Don't let someone convince you that your spirituality hinges on locking as many Bible verses into memory as you can. Your Christian discipleship is not about getting your head straight on a list of beliefs and propositions. It is a journey—a journey with the Lord Jesus Christ. The whole story of faith in the Bible is not an account of people sitting down and figuring out what they're supposed to believe. Biblical people are on the move. They are constantly moving through labyrinths of ambiguity, hardship, pain, ecstasy, and—for all we know—the serendipitous chase of an occasional butterfly. They go forward, trusting that things will somehow sort themselves out in the end. We could all afford to learn from them. And so could all the graduates who believe that everything they'll ever need to know is contained in the idea of goal orientation.

two mints

Every hotel room in America seems to have one of those folded cards from the housekeeping staff. We've all seen them, and, just as often, have ignored them. Typically, these mini "table tent" notices are comprised of some formal, preprinted message and then a line for the individual housekeeper to sign. If you're lucky, you get a smiley face drawn next to the signature. The card in my hotel room last week read: *It was my privilege to have cleaned this room for you.* A woman named Susan signed the card.

Since my wife's name is Susan, this little card caught my attention. I paused to think about exactly who placed it there. Who was this woman who cleaned hotel rooms, one after another, day after day? Was it really Susan who last cleaned this room? Or did Susan quit working for the hotel a decade ago and they just conveniently reuse the same card she signed long ago? What did this woman do for fun when she got to take off that Courtyard Suites uniform and be somebody else? Did she have children? How about a spouse? A home? A disease? A swimming pool in the backyard? I rather doubt the swimming pool. Anyway, I thought about these things as I opened my suitcase and inspected the bathroom.

My wife has tucked in a lot of sheets in her time, but she has never had to do it for a living. It must get old hunching over king and queen mattresses by the hundreds. Brutal on the back, would be my description. Then too, there are all the messes left by hotel patrons, some too gross to mention here. When I took a church group of forty high schoolers to San Antonio a few summers ago, they did a respectable job of cleaning up after themselves. A few needed more prodding than others, but the rooms were not a total disgrace. Still, I bet Susan would pick different words for her housekeeping card if she had a choice, were she the keeper of those rooms. A *privilege* to have cleaned?

For the first time in my life it dawned on me that a housekeeper might set out this little card as a matter of personal pride, not employee obligation. If a business card with your own name embossed on it is never likely to exist, and account executive, sales associate, and customer service representative are all titles beyond your future, this little housekeeping card is identity. It is your precious device for getting noticed in the world.

A middle-aged woman on the housekeeping staff at our local hospital always hangs out near the elevators. Her cleaning cart is nearby, as is one of those collapsible yellow floor signs—you know, the ones with the outline of a man being dumped on his keister: *Caution! Wet Floor.* The sign sits there all day, even though the floor dries in ten minutes. I'm convinced that my friend in the burgundy two-piece leaves it there to be noticed. It is her business card that declares, "I have cleaned this floor for you. Did you look down and notice?" She looks up whenever the elevator door opens. I always make sure to say, "Hi."

Before I left my hotel room the next morning for a day of meetings, I scrawled a quick note to Susan the housekeeper. I figure a note helps explain the tip and avoids an awkward situation for a housekeeper who doesn't want to be accused of theft. "Thanks for cleaning," I wrote. The five bucks were right beside it. When I came back that evening, Susan had left me a note: "Thank you. You're wonderfull [sic]!!" It was news to me that housekeeping staff were even allowed to communicate with hotel guests in this fashion.

I am not at all certain I am wonderful. But I am full of wonder for people who perform thankless tasks and still exude joy. Sometime later, I moved to prepare the bed. There were two mints on the pillow. I thought of those two ballpoint exclamation points pressed hard into my little letter of love.

unobtrusive grace

unobtrusive grace

the blue parka man

A middle-aged man in a blue parka snaked his way through the crowd on Concourse C. I got a good look at him from my front row seat near Gate C17, where I sipped my coffee and watched the passengers come and go. In Atlanta's airport, the whole world seems to shuffle by. You can glance any direction and see people of every shape, size, and color bump up against one another. Some are immersed in conversation. Some are walking against the clock. Others just seem lost in time, afloat in mental anonymity.

The man in the blue parka was different. He didn't have luggage on wheels. He didn't have a child clutching his hand. He didn't even have a ticket sticking out of his shirt pocket. He just had a Styrofoam box in hand—actually in both hands—a package he held close to his stomach. The box, which was the size of a little ice cooler, had a band of orange tape holding the cover tight. A big red label on the side read: "HUMAN EYE: Keep Upright at All Times!" This man was carrying a human eye right through Hartsfield-Jackson Airport, right through packs of people heading everywhere . . . and nowhere. Here I was all concerned with balancing my latté over an open book and this man was carrying someone's precious eyeball. In a flippant moment, I wondered if he had to put it through the security screening equipment. Can't you see the horror of the monitor attendant viewing a great big eye peering right back up at her?

The man slipped through a door marked "Employees Only" and headed down a flight of stairs. That's the last I saw of him. I didn't go back to my book. Instead, I began to contemplate who was to receive this eye. Who would be the lucky recipient? When would a certain man or woman, or maybe even a child, undergo the transplant? Where did he live? How long had she been waiting to see the face of someone who meant everything to her? I couldn't know the answer to these questions, of course. But from what a pilot friend who regularly transports organs had told me, I knew it couldn't be long before this eyeball had to have a new home. Someone would have the possibility of new sight in a matter of days or even hours.

It's hard to imagine the blessing of new sight unless one is well familiar with blindness. But if you think you are seeing pretty well today, don't be fooled. There are all kinds of blindness out there. Not every variety has to do with a retinal disorder. Jesus indicated that we are all capable of being blind to the truth. The apostle Paul regularly hung around people with 20/20 vision whom he believed were blind to seeing the light of the gospel. Maybe the greatest distortion of our sight stems from a spiritual misperception. We often don't see what we look *at* because we tend to see what we look *for*. In other words, we see only what we expect to see (or even want to see), which is its own spiritual problem.

Faith tells us that we can change the way we see. We can alter some of our visual limitation without a transplant. Seeing other people and places "as if for the first time" can release a fresh power in our lives. And when this sight comes through the perspective of Christ's own eyes, there is no telling how great this power can be. So take some time to think about what kind of vision you're after. Consider how you'd like to perceive a new world around you. And remember the dear soul who gets to receive a new eyeball and fresh sight, thanks to my friend in the blue parka . . . and the gift of someone else, who made it all possible.

synchronized discipleship

I have a friend who works as an occupational therapist in the neonatal intensive care unit (NICU) of a fine hospital. She is as good as they come, though she'll be the first to admit that some treatments require what medicine and therapists cannot deliver. Take, for example, the case of a premature baby's heartbeat, slightly off rhythm. Such a situation is obviously unwelcome. When intravenous medicines don't do the trick and the electric shock of a newborn's heart proves too risky, options are limited. What doctors have discovered is that sometimes skin-to-skin contact with the mother is the best way to re-synchronize the infant's heart.

The informal name for this beautiful bonding procedure of laying a naked newborn upon the bare chest of its mother is *Kangaroo Care.* It is derivative of kangaroos who carry their young close to their bodies. In the NICU, this means placing a diaper-clad baby—tummy to tummy—upon mother's chest. The infant's head is turned so that the ear is above the mother's heart. What often follows is a spectacular phenomenon. The less powerful vibrations of the child's heart begin to lock in step with the more powerful rhythmic vibrations of the parent's heart. In essence, they start to oscillate with synchronicity. NICU nurses and therapists have found that everything from sleep and weight gain to respiration and body temperature complications often can be helped by Kangaroo Care. When a baby gets cold, the mother's body temperature in a skin-to-skin situation may actually increase, as if to warm up the baby.

The scientific name for this cooperative phenomenon, when two objects or people want to "share the same frequency," is *entrainment.* A brilliant Dutch mathematician and physicist named Christopher Huygens made an interesting discovery in 1665. He put a series of pendulum-type grandfather clocks together in the same room, starting the pendulums at different times. All swung differently. When he returned the next day, all of the pendulums were swinging together. It was as if each had locked into the rhythm of another.

This mimicking behavior is more than a little fascinating. Entrainment is a good metaphor for how we might think differently about our Christian lives. What Christian does not want the faithfulness of his or her life to "vibrate" more resonantly with the heartbeat of the Lord Jesus? Who among us would not appreciate a bit more synchronicity with Jesus' impulse to love and serve? We all know the benefit of faith *in* Jesus Christ. But imagine the possibilities that would accompany having the faith *of* Jesus Christ—being so in tune with him that our words and deeds oscillate at the very frequency that is the Lord's own.

When John introduced the first disciples to Jesus and Jesus turned around to see them following, the Lord asked them a question loaded with meaning: "What are you looking for?" (John 1:38). What are you after with your life? What do you long for? What do you hope for? The disciples' reply was not what we would expect. "Where are you staying?" they asked him in return. In other words, What is your address? How can we remain with you? We'd like to move in and abide with you and learn from you for more than a little while.

To follow Jesus is to connect our humanity with his. It is to be with him. "Come and see," he says to his disciples. We don't get to move in residentially with Jesus, as those first disciples did. But this only means that our task to connect our humanity with those whom he loves is all the more important. Our assignment is to synchronize our lives with their needs. It is to see the face of Christ in them. For those whose poverty or want gives the pulse of a less robust heartbeat in life, nothing would mean more than if we who are not poor, who possess a more powerful heartbeat, would join them. Imagine if our abundance would lock in with their scarcity. Just picture the synchronicity—the pendulums of our very different lives swinging to the same frequency as Jesus.

biblical fundamentalism

When the Pilgrims left Holland in 1620, their pastor, John Robinson, offered words of promise and expectation: "The Lord hath more truth and light yet to break forth out of his holy Word."[5] Then off they sailed to the New World. The spirit of what Pastor Robinson articulated, that the Word of God is always revealing yet more light and truth than we know it to contain, is under constant threat. The threat is from a movement called *Biblical Fundamentalism*—a serious matter that divides Christians and destroys the liveliness of faith for far too many people.

Biblical Fundamentalism is that impulse to interpret the scriptures in a rigid way, fixating on the presumed literal and factual accuracy of every verse within the Bible. Such literalism eschews mystery and is threatened by ambiguity. It makes faith brittle and dependent on absolute propositional certainty. Instead of focusing on the truth of the story of salvation, a literal or fundamentalistic read makes the Bible a one-dimensional book, more useful for defending inflexible personal beliefs than anything else. Biblical Fundamentalism is based on a claim that scripture is *inerrant*, or without error. What this leads to in many adherents is the tendency to think and behave as if their interpretations are God-endorsed. Distinctions get drawn between oneself as a "true Bible-based believer" and other people whose beliefs are suspect because they don't line up with one's own reading of scripture. You may notice that a biblically fundamentalistic faith quickly assumes a punitive character. Fundamentalistic movements around the world are often described with words like *rigidity*, *domination*, and *exclusion*.

There is a widely held conviction among Christian fundamentalists that the Bible is God's only and final word. Instead of God still having something fresh to say each and every day by the power of the Holy Spirit, God's conversation with us effectively ended with the publication of the Bible. Thus, whatever a fundamentalist may deem a particular verse in the Bible to mean, that singular interpretation "settles it." There is no further discussion.

We should not espouse a worship of the Bible. Bibliolatry is a gross form of idolatry. Yet there is a lot of bibliolatry going around the Christian community. Our joy ought to be in worshiping the One whom the Bible reveals, not the book itself. As Jesus says at one point in his ministry, "You search the scriptures because you think that in them you have eternal life; and it is they that testify on my behalf. Yet you refuse to come to me to have life" (John 5:39-40).

If we treat scripture as a frozen body of ancient knowledge and literature, it is apt to become little more than a mummified word to capture our mindless devotion. Read in this light, a literal understanding of the Bible means we could still hold slaves with a very clear conscience. We could justify going into any country we might choose and slaughter any pagans we find. We could stone to death, under permission of the law, any woman taken in adultery (though, of course, men would be exempt).

This is not a biblical faith I want. The Bible is *holy* because it is so much more than a stuffy voice of the past. There is a holy hiddenness about the God who inspired it. This hiddenness means we must always be in the business of interpreting the scripture we seek to live. And, we need to interpret it with humility. As we inescapably bring our own passions and convictions to bear on any interpretation, we must acknowledge that no reading of scripture will ever be inerrant. We certainly do not have a stranglehold on the mind of God.

So, as a friend once said, "Beware lest the Bible interpret you faster and better than you can interpret it." Look for imaginative ways to read scripture so that your reading of it is not merely an echo of your own life. And receive the text as a gift that keeps accumulating meaning. For in so doing, you may find it has much more to do with directing your life in love than in serving as a prop to support your favorite interests.

add-on christianity

The cooking directions on a canister of Old Fashioned Quaker Oats could not be simpler. The only ingredients required for a steaming bowl of oatmeal are water (or milk), oats, and salt (listed as optional). Speaking on behalf of my taste buds, I say the salt is not optional at all. Unless a cardiologist tells me someday that it must go, I have no plans to skip the salt. That would be a mistake. It would be asking for blandness when richness is there for the taking.

We've all made the mistake of forgetting salt in a recipe. Or, maybe I shouldn't speak so universally—on a bad day in the kitchen, I can struggle to make a piece of toast. Last week was my moment with the salt. I sat down before a breakfast bowl of 100% whole grain oatmeal, hurriedly preparing to down it hot. Upon my first spoonful, I knew immediately that I was in the midst of a salt crisis. I had neglected to put salt in the oatmeal before adding the boiling water. Since the recipe calls for only *a dash* of salt, I tried again what I've tried before—grabbing the saltshaker and sprinkling salt directly on top of the cooked cereal. I stirred it vigorously into the milk and cereal mixture. For reasons that only chemists must know, it doesn't work well to do this. Salt on top is not the same as salt dissolved. I did eat the concoction, though none too happily.

My commitment to finishing that entire bowl of porridge gave me some thinking time. I started to contemplate a strange parallel with the world of Christian belief and practice. This is it: Christianity does not work well when added on top of an already full and committed life. Christ is either integrated into the fabric of our every day or Christ becomes an afterthought. There is no middle ground. Either we're at home with linking our lives to Christ as a matter of the heart, or we're practicing "add-on Christianity." If it's the latter, we become faith in name only, known by religious behavior that is more of an external duty, like "attending" church, than an internal, life-transforming, destiny-changing experience.

The signs of add-on Christianity are evident everywhere. Whenever we find ourselves using God or language about God to fulfill a particular desire or plan, watch out! We have added superficial markings of faith to a desire or plan that is essentially of our own design. Using God's name in this way is just that—*using* God.

Whenever we make sacrifices of a spiritual nature that do not draw us closer to God, Christ can easily become an afterthought. Some of us meet this tendency in certain Lenten disciplines that become self-serving ends in themselves. We spend more energy talking about some food or behavior we have given up for Lent than actually using the experience to deepen our relationship with God. Add-on Christianity can also describe the shape of our prayer life. I don't know what prayer I uttered when I sat down with that oatmeal last week, but I'm pretty sure it was hastily offered. Sometimes I pray with such little thought that I cannot even recall what I prayed by the time the prayer concludes. Have you ever had that experience? It seems especially common when we get tired or distracted. But these dispositions hardly make for worthy excuses. We're never too tired or distracted to eat the food for which we have just prayed.

Whatever such behavior is called, it is not the kind of spiritual life we want. It is not living steeped in Christ. It is cursorily sprinkling Christ on top of everything else we care about. It is appending the Savior to the surface of our lives. We end up with not only bland living, but also inauthentic faith. When Paul spoke of the astounding relationship we get to have as forgiven sinners in the heart of a gracious God, his language was not Christ *on top of* who we are, but Christ *in* us. "It is no longer I who live, but it is Christ who lives in me" (Gal. 2:20).

open your eyelids

In one his books, Philip Yancey tells the story of a young girl who used the power of her eyelids to shut her parents out of her life. Any time she wanted to make them mad, ignore their presence, or show repulsion, she simply jammed her eyelids shut. This meant that all the hand motions in the world from her deaf mother and father went nowhere but into thin air.[6]

One doesn't have to have deaf parents to relate. You know the disgust that comes when someone you care about walks away from you just as you're trying to establish a loving conversation or make a suggestion or, at the very least, update the kitchen calendar. It doesn't feel good at all. To be spurned is to be treated as irrelevant, to become the victim of indifference. It may be true, as Eli Wiesel has often said, that even something as ghastly as hatred is better than indifference.[7] At least hatred, as bad as it is, treats the other person as a person. Indifference turns that other one into an abstraction. Maybe you can remember a time when someone else's disdainful behavior made you feel like nothing. It's a lousy feeling.

I wonder if God doesn't feel lousy some days, the victim of our own indifference. Just think of the numerous ways God reaches out to us, constantly extending grace in our direction. Everything we enjoy depends on God and God's grace. Yet we live out so many of our days as if God does not exist and as if grace does not matter. God puts crocuses in front of our wintry eyes, needy people next to our bountiful lives, and soft-skinned babies in our arthritic hands. Yet too often we don't even notice God. We walk away from a potentially powerful conversation with the One who is brimming with a tender word of love. Other things distract us. We discourteously close our eyelids to what God is offering.

John Donne, the one-time dean of St. Paul Cathedral in London, once confessed from the pulpit, "I neglect God for the noise of a fly, the rattling of a coach, the creaking of a door."[8] We could update his 400-year-old language, but you get the idea: things get in the way. God becomes irrelevant to the organization of our day. We shutter our eyes to the very One who would love to partner with us in so many interesting ways. Remember Gethsemane? Jesus wanted to go off to pray, and in his troubled and sorrowful state, he asked the disciples to stay awake and keep watch. So what did they do? They fell asleep as soon as he rounded the bend and found a quiet place to pray. They closed their eyelids to the very One who cared so deeply for them.

Great wells of ink have been spilled over the centuries by people pondering the absence of God. Generation upon generation of people have wondered why God is not exactly in the place they would wish for God to be when they are in crisis. They may not inquire much about the presence or existence of God when the wheels of life are turning smoothly, but when things go awry, the Lord often catches the most heat. I have begun to wonder why we do not ask more questions about our absence from God instead of God's absence from us. Why should God be the only one required to make a command performance and show up according to our desires? Our absenteeism from the Lord is more than a little conspicuous.

So, before you neglect God for something that seems more urgent to you, try hard to keep your eyelids open. Look for things you've never noticed before. Watch for beautiful possibilities to ignite some new sensitivity in your life. And, most of all, remember how lousy it feels to be spurned by someone who is supposed to love you.

curvy lives

In my earliest days of theological training, I learned all sorts of Latin phrases. It's not as if they created inside of me some sort of instant excitement for ministry. Frankly, I could not detect any immediate value in knowing archaic expressions from another language. Yet something also told me that one of my professors was wiser than all my years, especially when he would say of a particular Latin phrase, "This is *really* important."

Incurvatus in se was one of those that would prove to be a lifelong treasure. In the sixteenth century, Martin Luther leaned heavily on these words—*incurvatus in se*—to conceptualize sin. We get all "curved in on ourselves," Luther argued, whenever we ignore God. It's a misshapen way to live. Our minds, bodies, and hearts get distorted, losing their open-armed, upturned way that signals a life in tune with praising God. We stop turning outward to our neighbor, instead curving inward to seek only our own advantage. It's a self-obsessed way of being.

One expression of this self-obsessed way is seen in our capacity to blame others for problems that belong only to us. None of us is blameless when it comes to shirking responsibility every now and again, but some people are especially clever at maneuvering their own problems into the laps of others. Five years ago a park ranger in Yosemite National Park told our family about a Bay Area woman who got stranded while hiking solo up El Capitan. During her attempt to reach the summit, a storm set in and she became lost in the fog. She dialed 911 on her cell phone and asked to be rescued. A helicopter found her only about a quarter mile from the top. When the helicopter lifted off and she saw the closeness of the summit, she asked the crew to set her down on top. They declined. She later sued them for kidnapping.

Or this: the Illinois State Toll Highway Authority is fed up with motorists who zip through electronically scanned Open Road Tolling lanes without paying. These are the high-speed lanes at tollbooths where motorists do not have to stop, thanks to a prepaid transponder mounted inside their windshield. A camera reads the little unit as drivers zoom happily on their way. The only problem with the system is its reliance on the integrity of motorists. There are plenty of people who would rather pretend to have a transponder than pay up. Last year, Illinois lost more than $15 million in unpaid tolls.

Fed up with losses, the Toll Authority has begun cracking down on scofflaws. The agency mails out nearly a quarter million delinquency notices every year, many of them with hefty fine assessments. Said one central Illinois resident who made the news, "When I got that envelope in the mail over the weekend, I didn't open it up until Monday. I knew what was in there. So I didn't want to ruin my weekend." But here's the kicker: what really bothers this guilty party is the accumulation of the fines. "I'm not saying I'm guiltless here," the man said to reporters. "But why didn't they stop me from breaking the law sooner?" Did you catch that? Here is a guy who honestly believes that it is the job of someone else to uncover his wrongdoing before he must rightly alter his crooked ways.

Incurvatus in se. It is possible to be so crooked in our posture, so curved in on ourselves, that we can't even see the path to righteousness. This is scary. But for all who are willing to pursue another way beyond their own way, there is the possibility of straightening out a crooked life. It's called grace. And God's grace is not simply the infinite supply of divine forgiveness for hapless lives. It is also, in the mind of Barbara Brown Taylor, the mysterious strength God lends human beings who are interested in learning to sin a little less.[9]

blue ribbon grace

Most spring track meets are built on speed. Special Olympics track meets are based on grace. You can take your pick as to which one gives you the greater rush. Personally, I'll pick the grace.

Last Saturday at nearby North Scott High School, there was an Olympic track moment, with special-needs kids and adults from all over eastern Iowa showing up to compete. Busloads of humanity huddled together on the football infield, clustered by their matching team jerseys. "Beijing 2008" can have the smog. Let North Scott have the magnificence of sunshine on a windy day. This day had both sun and wind in good measure. Beijing can have all the gold, silver, and bronze it wants. Let the Special Olympians in Eldridge, Iowa, have the blue ribbons. One little African American boy, who was all of eight years old, proudly proclaimed to me, "I won this ribbon all by myself." I could tell from his big, toothy smile that he wasn't lying.

When I first arrived, I could hear everyone shouting: "Hold on, Daryl! Hold on!" I cleared the bleachers just in time to see Daryl competing in the 100-meter dash all by himself. Here was this fifty-year-old man hobbling down lane three at top speed—"dash" can be a bit of an exaggeration at the Special Olympics. He was giving the stopwatch everything he had. Using remarkable dexterity while running, Daryl was gripping his pants at the waist, a fist on either hip. "Hold on" from the crowd had nothing to do with the lead; it had everything to do with Daryl keeping his pants from falling down.

Such was the spirit of the day, everybody rooting for everyone else. I had tears in my eyes during the eight-to eleven-year-old bracket for the 100-meter dash. One tiny eight-year-old girl with Down's Syndrome simply stopped walking about twenty yards into "the dash." I don't know if she smelled popcorn in the stands or what. But she wasn't going to budge. No cheering from the crowd would move her. Finally, another girl, a few inches taller and a few years older, came onto the track, grabbed her hand, and walked her to the finish line. The crowd went ballistic as these two slowly made their way. They weren't teammates. They were just brand new friends—one human being looking out for another one.

I noticed all morning long that these Special Olympians rejoiced in each other, regardless of what team they represented. It wasn't competition in the usual sense. The only thing they seemed to be competing against was that strange inner voice in all of us that creeps up and says, "You cannot do it. You cannot succeed. You cannot even finish what you set out to do." My own congregation had its share of competitors in the field. There was Selah and Brennan and Hope among them. When Hope crossed the finish line in her stand-up wheelchair contraption, her shoulders positively aching, she kept repeating a line that beamed the pride of a champion: "I did it." Hope is not a talkative young woman, which only goes to show you how carefully she selected those three words: *I did it.*

Hope did not complete the 100-meter dash with much form. But, she had all the grace in the world. There is nothing attractive in any conventional sense about dragging two feet that won't behave and propelling a body that cannot stand without assistance. But who cares about form? Planet Earth was without form and void when God first laid eyes on it. And yet look at the splendor we inhabit. Jesus had "no form or majesty . . . that we should desire him," according to some early musings of the prophet Isaiah (Isa. 53:2). And yet look at the grace he embodied.

The world is infatuated with speed. We obsess over form. But grace trumps them both. I found that out last Saturday, all over again.

ostrich egg

If you were a third-century Coptic monk living on the hot sand and beneath the big sky of a desert monastery in northern Egypt, your daily chapel routine might have included a curious sight. It was not uncommon for these monasteries to suspend an ostrich egg from their chapel ceilings. It was a tradition that medieval Italian painters like Piero della Francesca, Ercole de Roberti, and Luca Signorelli later incorporated into European altarpieces. Sometimes these eggs hung near a Bible. Sometimes the monks situated them between lit candles at the front of the sanctuary. They were always objects dangling high above the worshipers.

The idea of suspending an ostrich egg above the worshiping community was more than an odd decorative element. It sprang from the belief that ostrich eggs hatch in different fashion than other birds. Instead of the female sitting atop an egg, so the belief goes, ostriches hatch their eggs by staring intently at them from a distance. In fact, male and female ostriches are said to share this responsibility. If they take their eyes off the egg for even a moment, the egg is said to spoil and rot. An animal behavior professor might argue differently, but early Coptic monks didn't care as much about zoology as they cared about God.[10]

Herein lies the perceived value of monks staring at an egg. Their steadfast watchfulness was an imitation of the presumed vigilance of an ostrich. Every worshiper had the chance to contemplate the mystery of God with a particular, focused intent. The egg before their eyes was a form of admonition not to forget the mindfulness of the Lord for them. Faith has it that every time we look away from God, even for a moment's notice, we end up in trouble. We lapse into doing life our own way, that is, a sinful way.

The mindfulness of God watching steadfastly over us is a divine attribute calling for our notice. We could afford to learn from that loving gaze. When Peter turned away from Jesus three separate times, and the cock crowed, Jesus turned around "and looked straight at Peter" (Luke 22:61 TEV). It is that focused and undistracted gaze that gives mindfulness its uniqueness. Different from more intellectual sorts of commitments, *mindfulness* is a decisive act of the will. It does not want to waver. It wants to cherish again and again, like two spouses deeply devoted to one another. It stubbornly believes in sustained and loving attention.

God in Christ cherishes us regardless of the unlovable features that mark our humanity. This is the divine mystery, that God would be eternally mindful of us independent of our attractiveness. Victor Paul Furnish, a New Testament scholar in our time, put it this way: "God's love is not like a heat-seeking missile which is triggered by something inherently attractive in the target, the object of love."[11] Rather, it is the determined will of God to be mindful of us and fix a gaze of grace upon us that will not let us go. Like the psalmist, we could pray with perplexity: "What are human beings that you are mindful of them?" (Ps. 8:4) Or, we could just take the Lord's mindfulness to heart and honor it through our focus on others.

I heard someone say one time that if you want to have a ministry with strangers on the street that is worth anything at all, then walk slowly. This is the only way you will be able to look your neighbors in the eye and act as if they matter. If, however, you are not interested in anything more than talking about such a ministry on the street, then walk fast. You will be able to avert your gaze.

Staring at an ostrich egg has its devotional merits, I'm sure. And who are we to mock ancient understandings of incubation? But looking mindfully into the eye of someone who really needs us would seem to be the more Jesus way to honor the mindfulness of God.

ordinary grace

ordinary grace

mirror image

A big old yellow house sits on the corner of Grand and Locust Streets. It's close enough to the intersection to make it obvious that builders erected it long before Locust ever became a busy four-lane boulevard. The dryer exhaust vent pokes out of the east foundation wall. I never noticed this four-inch piece of PVC pipe until last Friday. That's when I stopped at the red light and spotted a young kid standing in front of the vent. He was a seventh or eighth grader probably on his way to school, and he'd stopped to warm his hands on a wintry morning. Or so I thought. The red light lasted long enough that I got to eye this middle-schooler for more than a few seconds. He wasn't just warming his hands; he was cupping them in the vapor, collecting just enough moisture on his fingers to be able to groom his hair. The storm window above the pipe served as his mirror. He tilted his head this way and that, capturing photogenic poses of morning hair that wouldn't behave. I was eavesdropping on a private moment in front of a mirror.

The sight reminded me of Norman Rockwell's *Girl at Mirror.* In that painting, a girl on the brink of adolescence, maybe eleven years old, sits on a footstool in front of a large mirror propped against a chair. Her chin is in her hands. She is wearing a petticoat. A child's doll has been flung carelessly to the floor. In her lap, perhaps replacing the doll that had just been there, is a magazine open to the photograph of a glamorous movie star. A comb, brush, and open tube of lipstick rest at the girl's feet. Her little-girl braids are pinned up in back—a gesture of longing for a more sophisticated look. Her expression seems to be a forlorn sigh, the critical survey of an image in the mirror that doesn't yet measure up to desire. It could be that this girl at the mirror is on her way to school hoping to look "just right" for the boy at the storm window. Or perhaps the boy at the storm window wonders if this will be the day when he'll get the gumption to say "hi" to the budding movie star with little-girl braids pinned up in the back.

"When will tomorrow come? When, oh, when, will tomorrow come?" This is the private prayer of many adolescents. But teens and pre-teens aren't the only ones who wonder when tomorrow will come. We all have the capacity to wait longingly for something to materialize in our lives that isn't coming in the manner we had hoped. Sometimes insecurity seizes our confidence in these moments. Nervousness can creep in. Disappointment has its own impressive shadow. I'm coming to the conclusion that the wisest thing we could do in such a time of longing is to not look in the mirror. In fact, put the mirror away. Turn away from your mug shot in the storm window and look into the eyes of the people all around you. Their faces will reveal more about who you need to be in this world than any primping or shopping will ever disclose.

So this week, take special delight in the facial expressions of all kinds of people. Notice more than you may normally be inclined to notice. If you're singing in church, unbury your head from the hymnal. Look up from your to-do list on the kitchen counter. Greet the eyes of the earnest teenager who is loading up your grocery bags. Wherever you go, be on the lookout for Jesus Christ, who promises to be hidden in the faces of people just like you—people longing for a life that doesn't always measure up to desire, people praying the same prayer I'll bet you've prayed many times before: "When, oh, when, will tomorrow come?"

holy amperage

There is a verse in the Bible that I have never understood. Well, there are a lot of verses in the Bible whose riches I cannot comprehend. But this one really hangs me up. I know it well because we always sang it in church when I was a kid: "For he is our God, and we are the people of his pasture, and the sheep of his hand" (Ps. 95:7).

Why doesn't it say what it ought to say: "We are the people of his hand and the sheep of his pasture"? Sheep belong in pastures—right? They're the ones that eat grass. We seem better suited for the embrace of God's hand. Even Isaiah prophesies as much: "I am the Lord, I have called you in righteousness, I have taken you by the hand" (Isa. 42:6). So what happened? Did some over-confident scribe take liberty when recording the psalm and assume that the rhyme or meter worked better to have people out in the pasture and sheep nestled in hand? We don't know. Scholars don't know. So, until someone knows, we just keep appreciating the poetic beauty of that line: *For he is our God, and we are the people of his pasture and the sheep of his hand.*

I'm fascinated by people who really know hands. Rheumatologists, physical therapists, hand surgeons, and blind people, to name a few, all know hands really well. They know them by their tough and callused outside and by their hypersensitivity on the inside. Not only do their lives or practices depend on knowing such things, so does much of the meaning they derive from life.

If you haven't thought recently about what it means or feels like when you hold someone else's hand or they hold yours, give some thought to it now. You don't have to be "in love" with anyone. You just have to appreciate the mystery and connectivity that goes with holding a hand. It happens at hospital bedsides every day. It goes on in high school football huddles. It's practically inevitable when people form a circle and pray. When you're finished reading this piece, why not hold one of your own hands under a bright light and just study it? Stare at that hand as you rotate it this way and that. Study it for the sake of its absolute magnificence, its architecture, its engineering. Gently manipulate the joints of your fingers and contemplate the designer who came up with such a contraption. It's an astounding work of art. Even if arthritis makes that hand hurt for you these days, it still is astounding.

I once knew an older gentleman whose job it was to hold hands with people undergoing eye surgery. I don't know what he was paid, given his minimal training and, in all probability, the need to keep his income below a certain Social Security threshold. But he treated every patient as if he or she was a brother or sister. His hand holding efforts not only lowered the blood pressure and the heart rate of the worried, it also reminded them of their humanity. It communicated the deep joy of another person caring enough to hold on.

Sometimes when I hold the hand of another person to pray, I think about very physical things, like the perspiration on either hand, or the size difference, or the shakiness, or the swollen joints. But most of the time, I just ponder the *current* that runs between us—a sort of holy amperage. I get lost, however briefly, in the idea that God would have a piece of my soul becoming a part of someone else's soul, and a portion of someone else's life becoming a part of mine. God is the source of that current, we discover over time—which may explain why, after all, we are the "sheep of his hand."

where is the sun?

Monday this week was like other recent days. Cold. Snow still on the ground. Too many days without sunshine aren't good for the brain—or for one's morale. It was another day without sunshine.

I climbed into my car and headed for the Dodge dealership. My car has a range of maladies, the most recent being a heater that doesn't work. I was amused—briefly—while driving home one night, that seven below zero outside (as my car's dashboard thermometer indicated) meant it was also seven below zero inside the car. The only difference was the absence of wind chill. The amusement didn't last very long as my hands nearly froze to the steering wheel.

Inside the service department of the dealership there was no sunshine either. The man at the desk put a piece of paper in front of me that indicated I would owe $90 for them to diagnose (translate: "look at") my car's problems. "You've got to be kidding? Ninety dollars?"

"Yep," he said. "That's standard."

"Does this fee apply toward the work if you do the work?" With the most convoluted of replies, he seemed to indicate that it would be included in the larger charge. The exhaust fumes were getting to me. I signed the slip.

I made my way to the service department's customer waiting area—a space the size of a large bathroom—where a young man was also waiting. As I sat down, we exchanged pleasantries in that windowless cave. *Oprah* was on in the background. The Coke machine's motor hummed loudly. Before I could open *People* magazine to catch up on lives I knew nothing about, he recognized me. "Aren't you a pastor at St. Paul?" he asked.

"Yes, I am," I replied.

"Is it Peter?"

"Yeah," I answered. Then curious, I asked him, "How do you know St. Paul?"

"Well, I've attended there several times." And with that little start to conversation, Greg and I were off and running. Greg's father, it turns out, had melanoma in its most advanced stage. He seemed eager to talk about the ravages of cancer and the Christian faith.

It wasn't long before a woman from the front office checked to see if we wanted coffee. She got involved in the cancer discussion when she heard what we were talking about, bringing mention of her own parents' plight with cancer into the picture. A stripe-shirted mechanic came in for a Coke. He heard what we were talking about and he too joined in; his father had just died the week before from cancer. I shared snippets from my own family's life, including my mother's death two decades ago from a brain tumor. There was not much sunshine in that room.

Here we were—four strangers jammed between Oprah Winfrey and a Coke machine running on one cylinder, talking about finite and infinite things. For twenty minutes we sat and stood there, carrying on. Greg wanted to know what I thought about all the cancer around and what role God might play with such a ravaging disease. He had big questions for a sunless day.

Here is what I think: for reasons beyond all comprehension, creation is deeply flawed, imperfect, and unfinished. None of us can make complete sense of suffering, even from the vantage point of faith. All we know is that God has no interest in managing or manipulating the details of our daily lives. While we may wish that God had written the complete script for our lives and that the earthly portion had a magical ending, who would want to be a part of a story that had already been told? If our lives were nothing but the mechanical execution of a predetermined plan, there would be no reason for faith. God opts instead for a different way. God gets mysteriously involved with our lives, even to the point of sharing our pain. And then, God transforms it all into love.

How does this mysterious involvement happen, and where does this marvelous transformation take place? Well, sometimes it happens in a dingy little room where the sun does not shine and where a motley group of people tries out their heartaches and hopes on one another. If you haven't had the experience, you might consider it. It could be worth the expense of getting your car repaired.

deep purpose

A seventeen-year-old high school senior in Pasadena, California, made national news when she did something remarkable. She achieved a perfect score of 800 on both sections of the Scholastic Aptitude Test (SAT) and a perfect 8,000 on the tough University of California acceptance index. Never in history has any student accomplished this intellectual feat. At her high school she was known as "Wonder Woman" because of her brains. Her college of choice is Harvard University.

What was interesting in the national news coverage of this young woman's story was a brief exchange she had with a reporter. Something possessed this reporter to ask, "What is the meaning of life?" Her reply was as memorable as her test scores: "I have absolutely no idea."

If that same question was put to any one of us, how would we answer? What is the meaning of life? Clearly, a coherent response would not require an exceptional intellect, but is bewilderment the only other option? When all is said and done in our lives, will we resemble the comic strip character who stumbles into a wall and wakes up with plus signs for eyes, stars swirling above his head, and the dazed expression of "what happened"? Or will the duration of days have accumulated some significant meaning?

If we are willing to take an honest look, we may see that our lives are starved for meaning. Maybe it goes without saying, but a decent job, comfortable housing, and respectable income do not necessarily add up to a meaningful existence. Not even world peace or a robust economy would amount to much for us if we lack integrity and purpose and are cold toward God. On many days, we grope for that which will make our lives count. We want our days to add up to something significant. We ask nagging questions that sound an awful lot like those of Russian novelist Leo

Tolstoy. "What will come of what I do today and tomorrow? What will come of my entire life?"[12] We want to know that our lives matter and that the world is somehow different—even a little bit different—for our having passed through it. Fame, comfort, and wealth are of limited help. They create as many problems for the soul as they do solutions. So where else do we turn?

Author Madeleine L'Engle suggests three options for how we might live our lives. The first way would be to live life as though it were all a cosmic accident, "nothing but an irritating skin disease on the face of the earth . . . a bad joke." The second possibility would have us walking outside at night, gazing up at the stars, and being impressed with whoever put the stars up there. The overall feeling we would be left with is that this One does not care one iota about us. Aloofness, perfection, and an indifference to creation would mark this One. The third option would be to live "as though [we] believe that the power behind the universe is a power of love, a personal power of love, a love so great that all of us really *do* matter to him." In fact, recognizing the magnitude of this one's love would give meaning to every single one of our lives.[13]

If we could live in this third way and take to heart the greatness of God's love for our every day, our lives would multiply in purpose and meaning. All those children whose pictures are not on anyone's dresser would start to matter to us. We would find a way to rejoice with the couple whose adopted baby smiles even bigger than they do. We would bother to pray for the widow who cries herself to sleep. And as for that homeless man who does a dance after landing his first real job? We'd stop and celebrate with him. This is the life that would be ours. Fresh meaning. Abundant joy. Deep purpose. Best of all—a whole lot of other lives would breathe easier because of the way we have chosen to live.

priorities in life

A lot of silent sizing up happens on airplanes. We enter that long tube of humanity and wonder what everyone else is made of. Who *is* that guy who seems to think he can shove a duffel bag the size of your average orangutan into the overhead bin? What's that young man in 3C reading that looks an awful lot like a magazine for female bodybuilders? Did my seatmate just rearrange the pocket in front of her because she's a neat freak or because she's positioning the sickness bag for a quick grab?

Just as I size up other passengers, I imagine they do the same with me. So, I'm courteous with my seatmates from the moment we board—or so I think—even initiating an introduction by name. Wow! Isn't that a bold move in this plugged-in world of marginal eye contact! After that micro-venture into hospitality, I figure I have done my part. That's when I turn my head and retreat into my own world of reading. I crave these rare moments of solitude. The chance to read a whole book or a stack of magazines—without interruption—excites the few "loner genes" I have. Normally on airplanes I avoid reading anything blatantly religious, fearing my seatmate may jump to one of those quick mental conclusions: "I'll bet he's a minister. I sure hope my husband on the other side of the aisle doesn't start cussing about not getting any food in flight or the nonexistent legroom." One too many conversations about "you-must-be-holy-and-kind-and-incredibly-compassionate-like-this-other-really-nice-young-minister-that-lives-next-door-to-my-sister" has scared the livin' daylights out of me for good. I don't reveal my vocation on airplanes unless someone threatens serious bodily harm.

Two weeks ago while flying, I hunkered down and climbed into the mind of Jimmy Carter, reading some articles by this former president. It was a pleasure to eavesdrop on a statesman with so much religious sensitivity. Much of the terrain he covers is implicitly biblical. Here is how Carter talks about what he considers the greatest discrimination on Earth—rich people against poor people—a discrimination he does not think is deliberate: "By rich people, I don't mean those who have a big bank account. I am talking about a person who has a place to live, who has a decent job or a prospect of a job, and who has a modicum of health care and some education . . . I am talking about people who feel like the police and the judicial system are on their side, and who think that if they make a decision it will make a difference, in their own lives, at least."[14] Carter goes on to say that poor people do not have any of these blessings. How many of us actually know poor people? If we do, do we know them well enough to go to their homes for a cup of coffee—or invite them to ours?

"We Americans live in a great country, the richest in the world," writes this former president. "[Yet] we're the stingiest country in the world among those that have a certain level of wealth. A recent poll asked American people, 'What portion of our annual budget do you think goes for foreign aid?' The answer, on average, was 18 percent. The real answer is .15 of 1 percent. Japan gives more foreign aid than the United States does for humanitarian purposes. So does France. So does Germany."

Carter then turns explicitly biblical: "Two thousand years ago, the people of Corinth asked Saint Paul . . . in effect, 'What is the most important thing in life?' Saint Paul gave them an answer that was hard to understand: 'The things you cannot see.' What are the things you cannot see? You *can* see a bank account. Is that important? You *can* see a beautiful house. You *can* see your name in the paper. But you cannot see justice. You cannot see peace. You cannot see service and humility and compassion. Those are the important things. And there was one more thing that Paul mentioned … and that is love."[15]

I finished my Jimmy Carter read. The plane landed and I got off. There at the baggage carousel, standing on the other side, was my seatmate. I began to wonder why I had lacked the gumption to start a conversation with her. She might have enjoyed the president's words as much as I did.

incentive morality

The local newspaper in our town carried a story about a nine-year-old girl named Jennifer who found an envelope containing $500 cash. Jennifer did what a kid with a good conscience would do. She returned the money to the bank named on the outside of the paper cash sleeve. One of the bank tellers recalled the transaction from earlier that same day and managed to pull up a check deposit receipt. The employee traced the money to its rightful owner and returned it to him. This, however, is not the end of the story.

The gentleman who lost the money ended up tracking down Jennifer and giving her five dollars in appreciation for the retrieval of his money. Five dollars is admittedly not a huge sum, at least in contrast to what was lost. But, then again, the man surely considered it a token of thanks, not some mandatory payment. One would think that returning property that isn't one's own, to someone else whose it is, would not be considered an action in the realm of the extraordinary. In our day and time, though, it seems such an act of honesty is increasingly viewed as extraordinary.

When Jennifer's neighbors heard the full story, a number of them expressed outrage at the stinginess of the man who gave a mere five dollars to the girl. They responded by taking up a collection among themselves. Within a week, they presented the girl with a $100 check. The card that accompanied the check explained their sentiment: honesty deserves to be recognized.

Now, here is a third grader who does the right thing. Her parents and others have obviously guided her well. But simply doing the right thing does not seem sufficient any longer, at least not in a lot of circles. We pay others for doing good. A whole system of incentives has emerged to undergird moral behavior and reward charity. I know of a high school student who receives $10 for every A he gets on his report card. One has to wonder whether doing well is its own reward. Doesn't an A on a report card confirm the joy of accomplishment and create its own good feeling? Parental respect, compliment, and affirmation would seem to be perfectly appropriate responses to a handsome grade point average. Praise has a way of extending its own good feeling and making its own contribution to value and dignity of another. That's what I thought.

Across the moral landscape, we rely increasingly on external gifts to reward the moral worth of our young. Kids receive new toys for behaving well. Parents offer their offspring money for honesty. Elementary school teachers dole out pizza as the prize for good reading. These rewards have become expectation in many places. Most of us don't even think to question them. We call them "incentives," believing that if we pay our youth for good moral judgment and behavioral rectitude now, someday the natural rewards for doing good will automatically kick in. But this reasoning has limits. If we're not careful, the next stage of incentive morality will be paying our children to brush their teeth and flush the toilet. Virtues like honesty, kindness, and integrity do not have an image problem that needs bolstering. They have a beauty that needs celebrating.

Jesus' idea of kingdom living is a world where goodness is good in and of itself and righteousness is its own God-pleasing activity. Preaching out in a field one day, Jesus told those who had gathered around that when they gave alms, their left hand had absolutely no need to know what their right hand was doing. In fact, he suggested that almsgiving in secret was the best way to go. What was he saying? There is no need to hunt for commendation. Be satisfied with God as your sole witness. Take care lest your desire for recognition slides into an obsession with vanity. It was among the more memorable sermons Jesus ever preached—and it still rings true for all of us who may be tempted to pay for niceness.

life's central melody

If you should get a chance to travel in the Big Apple any time soon, keep an eye on the toll collectors at bridge and tunnel entry points. Study their behavior closely. Read their lips if the din of traffic noise is too loud to hear what they are saying. See if they smile.

New York City has now hired lip-reading politeness police (a.k.a. undercover observers) whose sole responsibility is to check up on toll collectors in their little booths situated at the gateways to the Verrazano and Throgs Neck bridges and the Holland and Lincoln tunnels. What they want to hear are two words: *thank you*. Any booth operator who stands out as a grump will receive a citation. Those who enter the class of repeat offenders are in big trouble. It's not off to Alcatraz yet, but they would face disciplinary hearings before the Metropolitan Transportation Authority. MTA Bridges and Tunnels division authorities believe bridge and tunnel customers not only deserve a thank you, they expect one. Who knows what other cities are doing to enforce gratitude, if gratitude can even be enforced. New York City certainly has its own civility campaign.

I wonder if any of these toll booth operators have thought of taping scripture to their cash register as a reminding device. Colossians 2:7 comes to mind: "Be filled with thanksgiving" (TEV). On second thought, I'm not sure that would be my first impulse, holy as it sounds. My first instinct might be to post first aid suggestions for my boothmate, in case carbon monoxide fumes ever gassed me into unconsciousness. My second instinct might be to post clever comebacks for motorists who mouth off at me or who make snide remarks. Somewhere much lower on the interior decorating list of my little booth would be peppy reminders about offering up no-matter-what gratitude and good cheer for the cheerless.

I know this ordering of instincts is wrong. Gratitude and friendliness belong much higher on all our lists. Sometimes, it seems, we just have to shake a funk. We need to get outside our tiny box, or world, and get a larger view. Words of Dietrich Bonhoeffer come to mind for those fussy and self-preoccupying times of ours. "We pray for the big things and forget to give thanks for the ordinary and small things," he wrote. "How can God entrust great things to one who will not thankfully receive from Him the little things?"[16] Leaning out a window in freezing cold weather and giving change for a dollar is not what Bonhoeffer would mean by "a great thing." As a matter of fact, such an action is a very ordinary and small thing. Yet the expression of thanks through the little gestures of life is precisely what makes the world spin more beautifully. We may not need politeness police to tell us as much. But then again, unless one is steeped in regular praise for God's beneficence, how exactly would one know to take note of little things as if they matter greatly?

Gratitude is one of the most pleasant surprises in life, especially when it comes unexpectedly to our doorstep as someone's gift to us. Without gratitude we would miss out on life's central melody. We'd never hear the music of what God hopes for in our lives. We'd forget that we are receivers above all and before everything else. "What do you have that you did not receive?" Saint Paul asks (1 Cor. 4:7). Maybe *that* is the line that needs to be posted in my study, in your house, and in a lot of toll booths. If we had that melody in our head, we might just hear more than the annoying hum of traffic going by.

a poverty of relationship

While on a speaking tour in the United States, Mother Teresa of Calcutta remarked on poverty in America. Her great sense was that our nation's worst poverty was not monetarily based but relationally based. We have a serious poverty of relationship, she noted. Loneliness and isolation are rampant in our country. The more prosperous we become, the more disconnected we seem to get. This would seem counterintuitive since affluence opens up opportunity, at least in one sense, but we also know how prosperity can allow us to hole up with the illusion of self-sufficiency.

In the Book of Isaiah, the prophet denounces injustice when singing of the unfruitful vineyard. His commentary is as much social as it is economic, as he rails against those who build bigger and bigger estates: "Ah, you who join house to house, who add field to field, until there is room for no one but you, and you are left to live alone in the midst of the land!" (Isa. 5:8). Today in America, we have a crisis of living alone in the midst of our own land, regardless of the size house or apartment we occupy.

Part of our aloneness is directly connected to the disintegration of family traditions. Conversations about the breakdown of the American family are nothing new. All of us have heard reports, or contributed to them ourselves, of the increasing dissolution of important rituals and rhythms in everyday family life. Patterns that once kept parents and children emotionally and physically bonded are disappearing rapidly. What's more, new studies in the emerging field of social neuroscience demonstrate a clear linkage between relationships and physical health. Individuals with rich personal networks of family and friends and with high activity in social and religious groups tend to recover more quickly from disease. And, they live longer. One of the ingredients in our personal health is the flow of people through our lives with whom we get to connect and love.

I don't know if Mother Teresa noticed a poverty in Japan similar to our American crisis when she visited that country in 1981. Japan has its own problems with the breakdown of family life and the loss of relationship. Some entrepreneurial types have capitalized on this collapse. A Tokyo employment company named Japan Efficiency Headquarters has moved in to solve the problem of disintegrating family ties. For a modest $385 fee for a five-hour period, this company rents out single actors who play the part of absent family members. For $769, a couple can be rented for the same period of time. And, for just under $1,200, a rental baby or child can be included as well. It is a thriving operation, geared especially toward elderly persons whose families are too busy to visit. Lonely senior citizens who receive these mock family reunions don't seem to mind. Even though they know the participants are paid actors, evidently they prefer it to no family togetherness at all. You can hear the actors getting acquainted, can't you? "And you must be . . . let's see . . . mom?" Says the company's president, Satuski Oiwa, "Our purpose is to fill a hole in the heart."[17]

They must be filling a huge hole in the heart. Business is robust. Yet, what a sad commentary on life and the sanctity of relationship! There is no way to buy a relationship, or even rent one, at least not an authentic one. We cannot fabricate a relationship. Relationship comes through tender nurture and careful attention. It also comes through love. So, the next time you open the Bible to feed your faith, note one emphasis in particular: the gospel celebrates a relationship with a person named Jesus Christ above everything else—above doctrine, above knowledge, above even mystical experience. It's a relationship that cannot be fabricated or bought. It's one that cannot be rented. And all signs indicate that it's one that can never be taken away.

hyper-real people

The Nelson-Atkins Museum of Art in Kansas City, Missouri, has one of the finest collections of art in America. More than 33,000 works fill its galleries and storerooms. As a family, we visited there many times. The highlight was always the *Museum Guard* on the second floor. This 5'9" guard in uniform, whom we scrambled to see, was actually a sculpture—the work of Duane Hanson, arguably the greatest hyper-real sculptor in the world in his time.

Museum Guard stands watch in the gallery hall 24/7, hands folded politely in front of him. Art lovers from around the world study this man, talk to him, and inch as close to his face as they possibly can. If a museum-goer's hand or inspecting eye gets within four inches of the sculpture, a living guard immediately swoops in and asks for a step back. Sometimes I stood in front of the sculpture for as long as five minutes, honestly puzzled why this guard was not breathing. Every detail, from the complexion of his skin to the nostril hair and cheek mole is vividly real. Duane Hanson's work regularly fools gallery patrons. His sculpting process involves direct body molds of live models. He meticulously created three-dimensional people from casts of synthetic resins, later joining these different molds together. Selection of props, clothing, and hair followed. The whole process for one sculpture often took more than a year to fabricate.

If you stand in front of a Duane Hanson sculpture, you're likely to react like most other viewers: "This is so unbelievably real," you will say. "It could be me." You will want to talk to the sculpture because it invites you to converse. The resemblance to the living properties of your life will be that striking. Hanson's genius was to sculpt everyday people going about their everyday business. Whether it was a museum guard, a cleaning woman with a wastebasket, or a man on a riding lawnmower, each person he sculpted reflects some dimension of common life in America.

I noticed another effect that these hyper-real people have on me. They evoke a certain empathy. Locked in their situation, they sit or stand resigned to what they must remain forever. The ultimate paradox of this hyper-realistic art is that these lifelike figures seem unable to escape their circumstances. Their melancholic expressions never change. The museum guard stares into space, frozen forever.

When I think of Duane Hanson holed up in his studio to work on *Museum Guard* for months on end, I ponder the relationship he must have developed with this resin man. It had to be personal. There is no way one could work with a mold for that duration of time and not imagine a personality inside the polyvinyl acetate. Yet the liquid hardened. No living personality ever emerged for the sculptor to know, much less with whom to share life.

Just think how fortunate we are to have God as our sculptor and to be made of life and breath instead of mere resin and imagination. We get to be real before God, not just hyper-real. St. Irenaeus, the second-century bishop of Lyons, left us with some beautiful words: "It is not you who shape God. It is God who shapes you. . . . Offer him your heart, soft and tractable. . . . Let the clay be moist, lest you grow hard and lose the imprint of his fingers."[18]

To remain moist clay, we must constantly look for the image of God hidden within ourselves. A common mistake is to believe that God's image must be hidden in some other person but not in the ordinariness of me. So we overlook that divine image and end up dismissive of God's handiwork. Our hearts grow hard. We begin to lose the imprint of God's fingers if we look inside and see only a projection of ourselves. So how do we retain those fingerprints and that soft and tractable heart? It's all a matter of love. Where there is not love in the heart, no matter how real the life on the outside, there is not God.

surprising grace
surprising grace

galileo

I hadn't studied the night sky for a long time—that is, until I slept under the stars while rafting down the Colorado River through the Grand Canyon recently. Each evening, our kids would scope out a spot in the sand somewhere along the steep canyon walls. There we'd set up our blue cots. Bedtime came with the setting of the sun.

At dusk, the first constellations came into view: the Big Dipper, Centaurus, Taurus the Bull. Before long, the whole sky was packed with stars. It became difficult to see the major constellations given the saturation of heavenly light. The Grand Canyon is hundreds of miles from the nearest city lights. And you know what this means—no artificial lighting of the great heavenly mural that God unwrapped for us on the fourth day of creation. What an awesome sight! Here we lay beneath these inexhaustible riches of heaven. The vastness of it all. The thick Milky Way. The brilliance of small and big lights put up there by God. Genesis records their purpose: "To rule over the night." They certainly rule.

If you have slept on a narrow cot that sags between two aluminum rails, you remember how sleeping on your side is not much of an option. Lying on your back and staring up is the best way to go. This must be how Michelangelo received his inspiration to lie on his back and paint the Sistine Chapel. Our family lay on our backs beneath this great canopy of stars—a domed ceiling for a tentless experience.

Every time I would see a shooting star I'd thrust my hand toward the sky and say to my wife, "Susan, look at that!" She'd reply, "Honey, I can't see anything. I took my contacts out a long time ago." Then a slow moving satellite would cross the sky. I timed its course between the two canyon walls. Ninety seconds. "Susan, a satellite!" She'd reply with a touch of impatience, "Great. I can't see a thing. But I'm sure you're right." It was hard to be quiet in the presence of so much grandeur.

So, I'd tell her about still other landmarks in the sky. She came upon a refrain to quell the chatter: "Peter, dear, I trust you. I'm sure it's beautiful. But I took my contacts out." Eventually I rolled over and opened a book. The moon and stars cast enough light by which to read.

The book I brought along was captivating. It was a compilation of letters of the beloved daughter of Galileo Galilei sent to her father while he was under house arrest in the last decade of his life. The letters of Maria Celeste are touching and full of love for her father's well-being. More than anything else, though, the book makes clear the epic battle of the day regarding our rightful place in the cosmos.

In his earlier years, Galileo had rented a house in Florence with a high terraced roof from which he could pursue his nocturnal fascination. There he installed his lens-grinding lathes and made his stunning astronomical observations. The cosmology he inherited was that of Aristotle and Ptolemy. The Earth was said to be the immobile hub of the universe. The sun and stars bore the responsibility of orbiting around our little planet. The church of Galileo's time refused to budge from this earth-centric view. Psalm 104 was the proof that God "laid the foundations of the earth, so that it should not be moved forever" (v. 5 NKJV). Galileo loved God, the church, and holy scripture. But for the life of him he couldn't find a reason to dispense with God's gifts of common sense, intellect, and scientific discovery. The Copernican idea that Galileo embraced—namely, we are *not* the center of the universe, but rather spin through space and circle the sun—this was too much for Pope Urban VIII. Galileo was tried and arrested. His book was banned for the next two centuries. He fell into despair, went blind, and died in 1642.

The right hand finger that Galileo used to point to the heavens can be seen, encased in a gilded glass egg atop a pedestal at the Museum of the History of Science in Florence. It sits there as a testament to the night sky he revered, the same sky that still leaves us humbly looking upon its ever-brilliant light, whether we have contact lenses in or not.

astonishing tenderness

A 3.5-inch hamster and a yard-long rat snake made international news a few years ago when they found a way to happily cohabit the same cage in a Tokyo zoo. It wasn't intentional at all. Zookeepers could not find a way for the snake to grow an appetite for frozen mice so they tried a live hamster. The rat snake wouldn't touch the rodent. Someone at the zoo even named the dwarf hamster after the Japanese word for "tasty meal." That little joke didn't help. The two creatures were best buddies, constantly enjoying each other's company. The hamster regularly took naps on the snake's back. Eventually, the snake went for frozen mice. But he refused to touch his friend.

The world is not supposed to operate this way. Nobody brakes for butterflies. Hawks devour rabbits. Only Old Testament prophets talk about wolves living peaceably with lambs. We celebrate toughness. Our world touts it as a virtue. We build roughness into the game plan of life. Not that this is all bad. A police officer leading the vice or gang unit had better be tough or he may lose his life. A teacher in an alternative school needs something more than meekness when dealing with a hardened troublemaker. A hockey team trainer knows that relocating a dislocated shoulder or elbow won't happen by just talking to the arm of the injured. A certain degree of toughness is required in an unbending world.

But if we play too loosely with our penchant for toughness, we lose all capacity for treading lightly, looking tenderly, and listening carefully. Reverence for life begins to evaporate. One gesture of violence—it could be a bullet or a word—and life is gone. Jesus could be tough as nails when displaying a biting criticism of hypocrisy or righteous fervor against oppression. But it was his gentleness of heart that we're still trying to grasp for our own lives. Gentle is the one who does "not break the bruised reed or quench a smoldering wick" (Matt. 12:20).

One day in the Capernaum synagogue, Jesus of Nazareth was doing what he did best—opening the eyes of all to the power of scripture. The people were amazed. Their eyes opened wide as scripture came alive. That's when one sad creature, crippled by an unclean demon, climbed out of his pew and cried out: "Let us alone! What have you to do with us, Jesus of Nazareth? Have you come to destroy us? I know who you are, the Holy One of God" (Luke 4:34). Jesus called for silence and the departure of this demon. And then, in a surprising gesture of gentleness, the demon spirit placed the man at the feet of Jesus without hurting him—and he left. The spirit obeyed Jesus, said nothing more, and laid the man down at the feet of Jesus.

This "Gentle Jesus" is not the one people expected to encounter. They were eager for a "Warrior Jesus" who hated the Romans enough to defeat them. Theirs was a spirit of eagerness that still shows up every time we assemble a group of prayer warriors, publish a tract on spiritual warfare, or sing a battle hymn to trounce someone else. Many who live with cancer speak of waging a battle too. But many others, I have noticed, find an even better way to be at home with the cancer inside their bodies, enough to live life well without everything becoming an angry battle. There is an astonishing tenderness to their journey through hard times.

Gentleness has a surprising character to it. It will never hold center stage in our lives if we take too much for granted. If we assume we know every outcome, we'll miss out on huge chunks of life. Presumptuousness kills opportunity. It kills the opportunity for gentleness to flourish. I know that hamsters are not supposed to lie down with snakes. But if you always know what you are looking for, how on earth will you ever see what you do not expect to find?

surprise yourself

Summer is peak jump season in San Francisco. That would be for suicide jumps off the Golden Gate Bridge. Why July is the most desirable month for people to plunge to their death in the Bay is not clear. Perhaps there is some weird assumption that the water will be warmer, thus making this awful form of death somehow more palatable. But hats off to Kevin Briggs! He is the motorcycle patrolman who works the Golden Gate Bridge looking for people who are standing alone near the railing. An unattended backpack, briefcase, or wallet on the ground is a sure sign to him that trouble is imminent. Briggs is so good at coaxing people from jumping—he's talked more than 200 people from going over the edge—that the California Highway Patrol named him employee of the year a few years ago.[19]

What's the trick of Kevin Briggs? Among other things, he engages the potential jumper in a conversation as quickly as possible. "How are you feeling today?" he will ask them. This is followed by, "What's your plan for tomorrow?" If the person doesn't have a plan, he will suggest something like, "Well, let's make one. If it doesn't work out, you can always come back here later."

The majority of people contemplating a jump are struggling with depression. They're not crazy; they're depressed. Psychologists say that the most desperate ones view life as one long and unending rut. Briggs, who is no psychologist, has a knack for understanding when a life appears trapped by sameness and predictability. He sees his job as carefully trying to walk people out of this trap. Kevin Briggs's vocation of talking people out of taking their lives—which is so much more than a job—causes me to contemplate what it means to be stuck in a rut of sameness or predictability. Why is it that we often behave as if we have to know what tomorrow will bring? Tomorrow doesn't have to be the same as today. In fact, it may not be the same at all. Why can't we just embrace the possibilities that tomorrow might bring? The people on chemotherapy whom I most admire are those who, while they may be in the pits today, are open to the surprise of tomorrow. This is not to play lightly with the gravity of cancer or the complex disorder of depression in many bridge jumpers. It's simply to keep unpredictability and surprise from being ruled out of bounds.

One of the things God does best is to keep us from knowing what will happen tomorrow. We humans are pretty good at being inhospitable to the unexpected. We flatten out our universe. Why we operate this way is a bit of a mystery, but we do it quite regularly with the decisions we make and the cautious perspectives we hold. When is the last time you thanked God for *not* showing you the future?

We can't know what crossed the mind of Jesus on a typical day, but we can say quite unequivocally that his moves were unpredictable. To this day, we're still trying to make sense of how he picked his tablemates for supper. If the disciples were surprised that he frequently challenged the law, so are we. One didn't do this sort of thing and get away with it. He stunned the Pharisees with his daily unpredictability. Their whole religion was predicated on controlling the truth. They wanted Jesus to be the same as they were, which, if you think about it, is something of our own problem. It seems we're a lot more comfortable when Jesus feels the same way we do about stem-cell research, the posting of the Ten Commandments, or America's military policies. But maybe Jesus isn't into sameness or tameness.

It could be that one sign of grace-filled faith is a genuine openness to surprise, a willingness to believe that we do not know—and do not have to know—what is coming next. So surprise yourself and thank God for not showing you the future. You can be delighted by the wonder of what tomorrow may bring.

new spectacles

Everybody has a different definition of when the second half of life begins. Some people with children will tell you it begins when the children leave home. Others will argue that it begins when the first Social Security check arrives. Still others are convinced it starts as soon as you include aspirin in your daily breakfast menu. But these people are only guessing. I know *confidently* when the second half of life begins. It begins the day your eyes need bifocal adjustment. The second half of my life began yesterday. I'm absolutely sure of it. And the reason I know this is because I have new glasses with bifocal lenses.

Twelve months ago the optometrist indicated I was ready for this lens change. "It's your choice," he said. "You can probably go another eight or nine months without the adjustment if you want." Vanity and frugality told me I could ignore his prediction. My reading speed, which is very precious to me, began to decline markedly. So did the length of my arms. So this morning, I paid the tab and propped the new spectacles on my nose. I've been walking in a fog ever since. Ask me what it's like to be drunk and I will tell you. All you have to do is put on some "lineless, progressive bifocals," or whatever they call these costly pieces of plastic that dangle beneath the eyebrows and loop over the ears. Your world will begin to swim. Suddenly everything moves. In a normal conversation earlier today, I nodded a simple no to a colleague's question. That little twisting head motion sent my equilibrium into a tailspin; I felt like I was in a freefall skydiving maneuver.

In a few days, I'll learn how to cope with this new adjustment. I'll probably wonder why the whole world doesn't "get with it" and begin the second half of life sooner. I'll be trying to talk people with perfect eyesight into getting bifocals. But for now, I can't seem to escape focusing on little plastic lenses, searching hopelessly for invisible lines that connect heavenly sharpness with hellish blur. It's like driving from Chicago to Boston engrossed with the bug splats on your windshield instead of the view down the road. Don't try it.

Seeing, I've decided, is more than looking. We can look and look and sometimes miss something so beautiful or so obvious. Seeing is also about perceiving. The great seventeenth-century devotional poet George Herbert has a stanza in one of his poems:

> A man that looks on glass,
> On it may stay his eye;
> Or if he pleaseth, through it pass,
> *And then the heaven espy.*

Before you look up the word *espy*, I'll tell you what it means: to perceive or discover that which may be distant or obscure. Herbert suggests that we can either focus on a piece of glass, or we can treat it as a window and discover whole new worlds beyond—even heaven itself.

You know what it's like to see something with which you are familiar "as if for the first time." It can be something as simple as falling snow, an old friend, or some truth about yourself. But when you see something in a new way and in a new light, you are engaged in more than seeing. You are perceiving. You are discovering. So get those eyes checked. If you're halfway through life, make sure you wrap your good-looking face in some new bifocals. Then focus not on the plastic before your eyes, but on the great big world ahead of you. Let your jaw drop in wonder. You may just glimpse some feature of God's grace—even heaven itself—that you've never seen before.

the whites of our eyes

When the United States Congress passed the Civil Rights Act in 1964, the bill languished for months in the Senate because of a filibuster by southern Democrats. On the day that the bill finally came up for a Senate vote, every senator was present, including Clair Engle of California. Engle was dying of a brain tumor that had robbed him of his ability to speak. When it came time to vote yes during the roll call, he slowly lifted his crippled arm, looked at the clerk, and pointed to his eye. While this gesture signaled a link to the affirmative vote spelled "aye," it was also his eyeball sending a message. The message was that all segregation based on race must end.

We sometimes speak of our eyes as windows on the world. They behold. They take in. They receive. The New Testament spends precious little energy telling us what to do. It uses up a great deal of line space telling us what to see. Jesus does everything in his power to get us to notice what generosity looks like and see truth for what it is. He labors to convince us to see injustice and attend to the poor. The purpose of our eyes is to soak up the wonder of the world and pay attention to its hurts.

In the eleventh chapter of Luke's gospel account, however, Jesus utters a very curious statement about our eyes. Instead of describing our eyes simply as receptors, as instruments with which to see, he points out how they also are meant to be seen. They project something. Like Senator Clair Engle's eye in that famous vote, our eyes transmit important messages. Similar to lamps emitting light, our eyes deliver valuable signals to others. Jesus says, "Your eye is the lamp of your body"(v. 34), and "no one after lighting a lamp puts it in the cellar, but on a lamp stand so that those who enter may see the light" (v. 33).

When career placement pros coach job seekers on interview skills, they are quick to raise the topic of eye contact, and with good reason. Our eyes communicate our inside thinking outwardly, as much as they absorb the outside world inwardly. Of special note to researchers are the whites of our eyes. That portion of the eye surrounding the colorful iris gives off valuable information about what we are thinking, feeling, or about to do next. Watch the close-up camera work on an NFL linebacker sometime. It is the whites of his eyes that tell viewers where he might move in an instant. At a four-way stop, one driver's eyes go immediately to the whites of another driver's eyes, searching for clues on who will make the first move. It isn't the car type we notice or its passengers we study. It is the whites of the other driver's eyes. William Prescott, commander of the rebel forces on Boston's Bunker Hill, is famous for one line spoken to his troops as they were preparing for a charge from the British: "Don't a single one of you fire until you see the whites of their eyes." Maybe this was wisdom for an army low on ammunition. Or was it encouragement for the rebels to track their opponents' eyes in order to ascertain what they would be up to next?

Scientists in Germany have been studying the comparatively large whites of human eyes with the absence of whites in primates' eyes. One theory is that this darkness of eye in primates has allowed them to fool one another when looking for food. Their mates must wait for a movement of the head or body before they know to act. We human beings are different. The whites of our eyes give us away even when we don't move our heads.

The late theologian Helmut Thielicke was fond of saying that all compassion begins with the eyes. He wasn't just speaking about what our eyes see, but also what they communicate in their willingness to reach out to a hurting world. "Your eye is the lamp of your body," says Jesus. That eye exists, in part, to emit grace and project compassion to a world scanning the horizon for signs of hope.

advanced radiology

Recently I conducted the memorial service for a thirty-eight-year-old radiologist. He was killed when his car slid off Interstate 80 in a snowstorm. The only good that comes from an experience like this, when a life ends so abruptly, is the inspiration that it often creates for survivors who want to organize their lives in a new way. There in the hospital chapel, I visited with nurses, technicians, physicians, and classmates of Jason. As each of them spoke of his ability and intellect, it became something of a primer for me in what makes for a good radiologist.

I learned that good diagnostic radiologists must be at home with all sorts of imaging equipment these days, especially Magnetic Resonance Imaging. They need to be excellent interpreters of information, confident in their medical knowledge, and well familiar with anatomy, chemistry, and biology. They have to be ready to perform under pressure with a keen sense of judgment, often when a life hangs in the balance. Oh, yes, exceptional eyesight is also a big plus.

Meet John Somers of North Platte, Nebraska. He never went to medical school, much less entered a residency program in radiology. Yet he has the gift of diagnostic excellence. He can interpret films like few other locksmiths in the land. That's right, he's a locksmith. Some time ago, Mr. Somers received an urgent call from an individual in crisis. A man named Arthur Richardson was on the other end of the phone. The story behind the locksmith-turned-radiologist began as a joke. Arthur Richardson thought he would play a trick on his friend and pretend to swallow the friend's pick-up truck key. The prank backfired. Richardson accidentally swallowed the key. He must have some super-sized gullet. Every pick-up truck key I've ever seen is large, with a beefy plastic grip. The friend had no spare key for the truck, so the two traipsed off to a doctor. Richardson received a stomach X-ray and took his films to the local locksmith.

"I've done all sorts of lock work. I've done all sorts of safe work," said John Somers. "This is truly a first in my career." He used the X-ray images to fashion a new key. And it worked. The pick-up truck actually started. The local hospital may hire Somers if he's not careful. He's one darn good radiologist.

In biblical imagery, keys are recognized as symbols of power and authority. They are associated with power because they are given to persons who are judged to be trustworthy. Thus, responsible stewards whose character suggests responsibility are the ones rewarded with the possession of keys. Relative to that which it can open, a key is quite small. Whether it opens a temple door or starts a pick-up truck, a key's comparatively small size also suggests something of power and exclusivity.

The most famous passage in the New Testament involving keys is Matthew 16:19. In it Jesus empowers Peter with the keys of the kingdom, evidently relying on the twin themes of trust and responsibility witnessed in this disciple. Through his confession of faith, Peter seems to grasp who Jesus is, implying that he is capable of being trusted with the keys. Now, while we may want to note the apparent absence of responsibility in Mr. Richardson, we should not forget Peter's own fickleness and undependability. He demonstrated his own irresponsibility with the power of keys when he denied knowing Jesus three separate times.

According to the New Testament, human beings have been entrusted with the authority first ascribed to Peter—to set people free with the power of the gospel. If you wonder what we need to be freed from beside sin, it may depend on the day. Arthur Richardson appears to need more than the gospel at the moment. Last I heard, the truck key was still inside of him. He tried to vomit it up. Then he drank milk of magnesia to flush it out. Neither worked. Whatever his next steps are, they may well be beyond the medical wizardry of John Somers, superb radiologist that he is.[20]

digital time

I have skimmed *The Complete Idiot's Guide to Managing Time* (New York: Alpha Books, 1995) enough to learn a few importantly useless facts. Over the course of a lifetime you and I will spend at least five years waiting in lines. We can look forward to spending eight months opening nothing but junk mail and six months staring at traffic lights that won't turn green fast enough.

Managing time is not an irrelevant exercise. The way we manage time has a lot to do with how we manage our lives. Like most people I wear a little object around my wrist to remind me how to live life rather than let life pass me by. I do know a few people who pretend they have no need for clocks or watches. But sustaining a web of relationships that involve virtues like accountability and dependability must be tough without some device for telling time.

Recently I took out a ballpoint pen to reset my daughter's purple digital watch. Fighting to reset that cantankerous watch brought back the question I have asked before: Why did someone bother to invent the digital watch? Time displayed as printed digits seems to do weak justice to the splendor of time. The numbers mysteriously appear as if in a vacuum. The little square-cornered digits present no circle as a reminder of the rotation of our planet. They offer no connection with past or future. In fact, without some mental computing in one's head, a digital readout gives no indication where we've come from or where we're going. All it allows for is a numeric abstraction called "now."

The analog watch, by comparison, is organized around a circle. It is a circle that acknowledges the cyclical time frame that envelops every day. By definition time is indebted to the rhythms of the earth and the solar day. As the planet rotates, so does time, giving us a way to reference past and future. The distinction between analog and digital time is significant for crafting our lives. The former hearkens back to a premodern age when time was tied closely to experiences connected with natural points in the day. The latter prizes numbers in the abstract.

I wonder about kids—or adults, for that matter—for whom the idea of organizing time is a total abstraction. If we live more in the world of virtual reality than natural reality, and our computers' nanosecond behavior gives us the attention span of a gnat, how will we ever learn to *feel* time? We may find ourselves struggling to experience it fully. It will exist more in a vacuous realm beyond personal awareness.

This is no call to throw away your brand new digital watch. But think, for example, what a round clock announces when its hands rotate past the midnight hour. In that moment of handing over a brand new day, God is giving a fresh chance for us to be more in touch with time. It's God's offer to help us tie our lives more tightly to the experiences of the day. It's an invitation to notice the circadian rhythms of nature and the biological turnings within us.

My watch does not help me manage time. But the steady movement of its hands around the circumference of a circle reminds me that a really good life is always organized around a center. A well-lived life revolves around a fixed point. Much like the way the gravity of the sun holds the planets in orbit, so the gravity of God holds us through the evolutions of our lives. God becomes the fixed point to which the rhythms of all creation owe their existence.

So imagine what life might look like if we gave even a little more attention to appreciating this gift of time according to a circle. We'd probably catch ourselves watching finches at the bird feeder more often, enjoying children playing happily in supermarket aisles, and pulling over our car to take in more sunsets. A watch may be nothing more than a timepiece. Then again it could be the very instrument that helps us organize our lives more closely around a holy center bearing the name of God.

the whole enchilada

Some few years ago, *Sky and Telescope* magazine organized a national contest to rename The Big Bang. There was no prize money involved, which only goes to show the personal satisfaction that one must derive from dreaming up a new name for creation. When is the last time you received such a cosmic honor? Readers submitted nearly 13,000 ideas. Heavyweight personalities and brilliant scientific minds, the likes of Carl Sagan, served as contest judges. In the end, the judges found no suitable replacement to trump their preference for The Big Bang. There were plenty of honorable mentions. I would have been proud to think up any number of them myself: Bouquet of Beginnings. Doink. Go God! Jiffy Pop. Let There Be Stuff. Okay . . . Fine. Bursting Star Sack. It's a Universe. Hey, Looky There at That. Leisurely Cosmic Expansion. Infinity Forever. The Primal Billowing. Well, I'll Be! The Whole Enchilada. Bob. Wouldn't that be something if the event or theory that supposedly created our universe was renamed Bob! Picture the jolt of self-esteem for all the Bobs around the world.

Recently, I did something I've never done before. I went on a third grade field trip. Our destination was the local high school planetarium. Our purpose was to view some moon rocks. Twenty-two nine-year-olds sat with their coats on in the dimly lit room, wondering with the instructor why the heat wasn't working. At first, the kids seemed more interested in the tilt seats that squeaked with every move than in the instrumentation all around us. But when the lights went out in that round room, the squeaking stopped. The movie began. First it was footage of Cape Canaveral, 1969. Then it was clips of the first lunar landing. All was quiet as every little eye zeroed in on the spacecraft lowered down to the moon's surface. Stars from a separate video projector in the planetarium lit up the domed sky on the ceiling above. We were in outer space. I thought of Madeleine L'Engle's line:

"When I need a dose of wonder, I wait for a clear night and go look for the stars."[21] It was ten o'clock in the morning, with a room full of third graders tilted back in tall seats, but I felt a little dose of wonder.

The camera zoomed in on the footprints of Neil Armstrong and the hopping motions of "Buzz" Aldrin, who looked remarkably like an inflated rabbit. The kids started to *ooh* and *aah*. I listened for one of them to say, "Hey, Looky There at That," or "Check out that Leisurely Cosmic Expansion," or "Is this part of Jiffy Pop," or "Doink." I didn't hear anything of the sort. But through their expressive sounds I could tell they were taking in a piece of the whole enchilada with no small measure of awe.

The moon rocks we saw that day, if the truth be told, were really specks of moon dust layered in inch-thick clear acrylic slabs. As the kids stood in line to view this undramatic sight through a microscope, it was clear that the knobs on the scope were more interesting than the dust particles beneath the lens. I assumed the job of refocusing the microscope for each pair of eyes, while out of the corner of my eye, I watched this amazing teacher calmly work the room. As the kids roamed all over, touching every instrument, poster, and object in sight, I discovered again my deep respect for really gifted teachers. Here was a science instructor who obviously enjoyed children and who loved to teach. How else could he handle their delightfully odd questions so beautifully and their hands moving all over the place?

Before long we were back on the bus, breathing diesel fumes again. I stared out the window and saw no stars. It was 10:45 A.M. Somehow, though, I knew I had been in the presence of awesome mystery just moments before. I could still hear the sounds of those happy kids in that domed room, discovering the heavens. As for the teacher's part, I was certain that his gift for expanding the imagination of others was nothing short of magnificent.

mysterious grace

mysterious grace

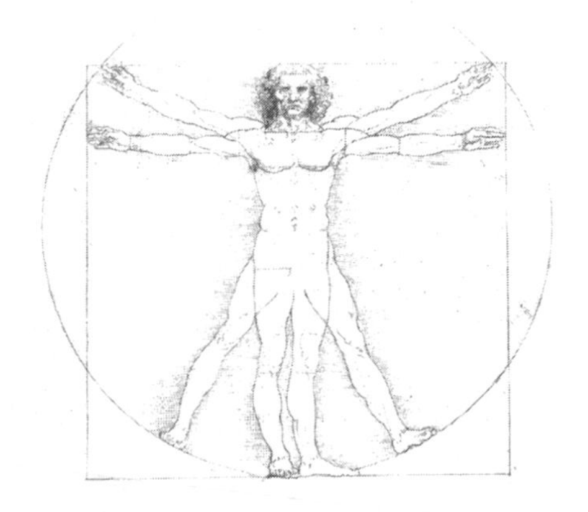

ambidextrous faith

I have a new hero. He is twenty-one years old. Creighton University junior Pat Venditte is making national headlines as a two-armed pitching phenomenon. That's right, he can throw a fastball or a curve ball with either his right or left arm. It is something to watch. To left-hitting batters, he winds up left-handed and to right-handed batters he throws right-handed. He can deliver a ninety-one-mile-an-hour fastball or a biting slider. Name your pitch.

To those who wonder how he does it, it all goes back to his life as a toddler. Pat's father encouraged him to throw with either arm. He has ever since. Today he wears a specially made glove, odd in appearance. Four fingers are flanked by two thumbs. He can slip it on either hand with quick ease. In nearly seamless fashion, he can rapidly change throwing arms, often causing fans to do double-takes.

Switch-hitters are a common commodity in baseball; switch-pitchers are a rarity. Only one major league pitcher in the last century displayed this prowess, and even then it was more stunt than strategy. Venditte's talent has its humorous side. When pitching against Nebraska last year, he faced a switch-hitter who came to the plate as a right-hander. When Venditte shifted his glove to pitch right-handed himself, the batter quickly moved to the other side to bat leftie. This prompted the pitcher to do the same. After this circus play of back-and-forth maneuvering, the umpires finally stepped in and made a ruling: the pitcher must declare which arm he will use before throwing the first pitch. There is no changing while the same batter is up to bat.

Pro scouts are watching Pat Venditte closely. Even though the trend in baseball is toward specialization, Venditte's versatility could offer an economical two-for-one savings. What's more, he has a looser pitch limit than his peers since both of his arms can share the workload. We probably haven't seen the last of this young athlete.[22]

Pat Venditte is my hero because what he does ambidextrously with his arms is exactly what I want to do with my faith. I want to get rid of the lopsidedness that informs too much of how I live and speak of faith. Perhaps you have noticed how we tend to favor one good side, of two, on so many spiritual matters. Consider almost any subject and the unevenness shows up. Prayer is a perfect example. We can pray with great fervor for something, and if our prayer request happens to get satisfied, so much for the deep and continuing prayer life. It's as if we cannot hold the blessing of God and the blessing of material good even-handedly together. At least it's hard without unintentionally overlooking the other. As the old African proverb has it, "When I pray for bread and get it, I think about bread and forget God. When I pray for bread and don't get it, all I think about is God."

Or take the contemplative life in contrast to the more active life of service. How can one observe both at the same time? The minute we settle seriously into a contemplative mode, we risk ignoring our critical role in a world of hurt. Yet if our greatest effort plunges us constantly into the desperate needs of others, what will happen to adequate and equal time for nurturing the contemplative life?

Do I as a pastor spend my greatest amount of energy focused on helping hold together the splendid intricacies of a Christian congregation? Or, do I spend the bulk of my time out in the wider world, excitedly with people who do not know church, "get" church, or are hostile to church, and thus lessen my own attention to nurturing the home front? How can we have it both ways? The Pharisees, we recall, had certain faith practices like tithing all figured out, but they missed others altogether, in part because of their zeal to tithe.

I don't have an answer to this spiritual laterality—this preference for one good way over another. On any given day we are all guilty of favoring one side of our head or heart over the other. It may be that we all need to sit in the Creighton University's bleachers for a day and quietly learn from that twenty-one-year-old who has mastered ambidexterity like few others.

in the twinkling of an eye

I do not put people into categories casually. Most attempts to bundle human beings and pigeonhole them into like-type groups, just to make easy sense of the world, strikes me as wrong. Too often, it's a practice that leads to exclusion. But some distinctions are fair and non-exclusive. I made one recently. It follows years of observing people who transition from their own home into some kind of retirement community or care facility. What I have concluded is that there are basically two kinds of persons living in such places. One variety takes all the blessed experiences they have been given in life and turns them into a new vision for happiness. These are forward-looking people who do not measure the significance of their joy by their surroundings, but by the knowledge that the gift of every new day is just that—*new* and *a gift*. The other variety of folks are individuals who expend great energy calculating what they have lost. They lament "what is no more" in their life. The transition to a new home is excruciating for them, and they chase contentment by trying to relive the past.

The human journey is so short. We no sooner figure out why we are here than it is already time for us to be leaving. We get caught between the irreversibility of the past and the unpredictability of the future. Life becomes a long string of good-byes and hellos. As we get this good-bye and hello rhythm down, we find that accommodating change comes a little easier. We stop trying to live a remembered past, and we start to drink more deeply of the "now." Every moment begins to shine with a quality that cannot be purchased. We experience each new day with the excitement of the first time. This very day is, after all, a gift. And it is new.

Few people shed tears when they must say good-bye to an inanimate object devoid of relationships. Watching one's rusty Buick get towed to the junkyard rarely evokes tears of sorrow. But a congregation saying good-bye to its beloved sanctuary, now replaced with a new one, is another story. A family that bids a heartfelt farewell to Mom just before she breathes her last knows the pathos of a human good-bye. Taking stock of a past that is unrepeatable and a future that is unknown is an emotional experience. Count on a few tears. They belong with every honest good-bye and exciting hello.

As I write this essay, my wife Susan and I are preparing to drive our firstborn to his opening semester of college. I'm guessing we'll use most of the 1,310 miles between Davenport, Iowa, and Waterville, Maine, to ponder what happened to eighteen years. Just yesterday, Jacob was three years old standing on tiptoes at the living room window, bursting with an excited smile, waiting hours on end for his grandparents to pull in from out of town. The Bible says our transition from death to resurrected life will be as fast as the twinkling of an eye. I wonder what this makes a son's transition from three years old to young adulthood.

I don't have the good-bye and hello rhythm down perfectly anymore than you do. But I know that I want to be the kind of person who takes all the blessed experiences of the past and turns them into a new vision for happiness. I want to be as excited about the unknowns of our children's next chapter as I am appreciative of their last. So my word to you is the same word I want to give myself: "Live this day as if it were your first day, as if it were your last day, as if it were your only day." And for goodness sake, don't hesitate to cry. Every honest good-bye and exciting hello deserves at least that much.

specializing in reverse

India and Pakistan do not love each other. There is deep chill between these South Asian powers. Ethnic rivalries and territorial disputes have brought out the worst in them. Both nations engage in intense propaganda and psychological warfare. They regularly toss out each other's diplomats, considering them little more than a cover for spies. Dangerously so, they happen to be nuclear rivals too. So how does one ever conceptualize a future of peace and harmony between these two powerful nations? It may require some very unconventional method.

Harpreet Devi has such a method in mind. He is a taxi driver in the Indian state of Punjab. Several years ago, his life changed dramatically when his taxi's transmission broke. Actually, it wasn't a total breakdown; his car simply refused to go forward. Devi had no option but to drive home in reverse. He has been driving in reverse ever since that day, benefiting from a special dispensation from the chief minister of Punjab, who has put a halt to police stopping Devi for this odd driving practice. The transmission malfunction gave Devi the idea for an entirely new philosophy in life that he calls "specializing in reverse." The idea is that one can improve a situation by "going into reverse." In his case, the situation he most wants to improve is the relationship between India and Pakistan.[23]

"I don't have a video screen or a radar on my dashboard," he told a BBC reporter. "So, I have to turn around to drive." He has modified the forward gears in his taxi so they now work in reverse. Additionally, there are now headlights in the back of his car to alert other motorists to the direction which he is traveling. All of these adjustments help serve the goal of his philosophical approach to gaining peace between his country and Pakistan.

Harpreet Devi regularly drives in reverse at speeds up to 85 kilometers per hour and expects soon to be going 100 kilometers per hour. It's not without some physical pain. "I have got a severe backbone problem from driving so fast in reverse, because my whole body gets contorted. . . . I do have frequent pains in the neck, and I have had severe vomiting." Does he consider the pain worthwhile? Absolutely. "To achieve something, you have to do something." He also has had some near misses in the crash department. "By God's grace," he reports, "I was okay." Devi is confident he can make a difference, promising to bring his "going in reverse" philosophy to other troubled spots in the world once he succeeds in bringing India and Pakistan closer together.

If Devi's method for making a difference sounds preposterous, it is. His commitment to driving in reverse is "absurd," "ridiculous," or "completely senseless," all of which happen to be accurate definitions of the word *preposterous.* Preposterous is indeed a strange word. Etymologically, the prefix *pre* means, "that which comes before." The body of the word, *posterus* (in Latin), means, "comes after," or "behind." Thus, the literal sense of the word *preposterous* is "what is before comes after." The basic idea is contained in our idiomatic phrase,"the cart before the horse." Preposterous activity is absurd, backward, reverse.

The Christian faith is preposterous. It asks us to live in ways that the world considers absurd and backwards. People who are interested in following Jesus recognize sooner or later that certain priorities must go before other ones. They know that the last are supposed to be first and the weak come before the strong. They know that neighborliness is next to Godliness. They know that "collateral damage" is unacceptable to peacemakers. They know that children are the best thing this world has going.

How do they know all of these things? Because Christ's people *specialize in reverse.* They cherish the idea of throwing life's transmission in reverse and looking out the back window. They don't mind a crooked neck so long as their values are straight. They're just busy trying to keep up with Jesus.

sleeping lightly

If you are experiencing stress in your life, you may be sharing good company with Jesus. There is a fascinating biblical story that seems to highlight stress in his life. We find it in Mark 1:29-39. People were swamping Jesus with requests for his ministrations. To many local folks, Jesus seemed an exotic physician helping a town that lacked adequate healthcare. The whole city of Capernaum gathered at the doorstep of Simon and Andrew's house. They wanted Jesus to touch them. Friends not only brought sick people to Jesus; they kept on bringing them, even after the sun went down, says Mark.

Historians do not know the population of Capernaum at the time. All we know is that "the whole city" showed up (v. 33). Jesus did what he could to heal the various diseases that people put before him. But at some point he did what must have felt necessary—he closed the front door and went to bed. There were too many patients for too few appointment slots. Besides, the people were missing the point. Jesus wasn't out to be some new medicine man. These random healings were only supposed to be signs of the kingdom of God, not the announcement of a new hospital opening nearby.

If we look closely at the biblical text, we notice that Jesus got up before sunrise. "Way before dawn," the original Greek manuscripts suggest. There may have been so much on his mind that he could not sleep soundly. Whatever the case, he tiptoed out the back door, off to clear his mind and gain new strength through some pre-dawn prayer. He found a secluded place to pray. Back at the house, something awakened Simon, perhaps a sixth sense that Jesus' bed was empty. He went searching for Jesus, and when he found him, told Jesus words he probably preferred not to hear: "Everyone is searching for you" (v. 37). Jesus tells Simon, in effect: "Let's get out of here. And now! On to the next town where I can keep doing what I came to do."

We have all been there. Restless sleep. Too much on the mind. Thoughts of caring for others that have no end in sight. Friends and neighbors in crisis, whom we worry about. All these concerns have us sleeping lightly some nights. Well, as it turns out there may be good medical reason for this. A brilliant twenty-one-year-old undergraduate at Johns Hopkins University has made a startling discovery. Serena Gondek presented her findings to the American Academy of Neurology. What this suburban Chicago woman discovered through laboratory experiments was that part of the brain stays awake even when we sleep. A frontal lobe portion of our brain does not rest as it decides which noises and thoughts are serious enough to demand we be awakened.[24] It all makes sense. That lobe mysteriously monitors something of our environment while we sleep. Mothers of newborns will testify to this. They can hear the slightest whimper, yet sleep through the roar of a freight train. It's the sort of vigilance system of sound and thought processing that might have kept earlier humans from being attacked and eaten.

Is it possible that Jesus of Nazareth was so distracted on some days by the hopes and needs of hurting people around him that he could not sleep well? Yes, it's entirely plausible. Human need and anguish work on the human spirit this way. Compassion for the predicament of other people gets into our brains. We lose sleep over situations that weigh heavily on our hearts. We sleep more lightly. Who knows if the stress we live under heightens the brain activity of that vigilance system or if sleep deprivation heightens our stress level? Either way, I'm glad to have something to blame for my anemic sleep on Saturday nights. I twitch in panic during that night of the week, fearing that I have missed the start of the very worship I am supposed to lead, misplaced the sermon I am supposed to preach, or mistakenly set the alarm on which I am supposed to depend. It's an awful feeling. Now, at least, I have a frontal lobe to blame.

blessed are the poor

The congregation I serve is not overflowing with poorly educated, unemployed, homeless, mentally ill, and physically challenged people. While there are some of each type, most of us are well-fed, well-educated, and well-supplied. You can argue degree, but you're apt to find that your starting point for arguing still originates from a personal situation of relative comfort. The people with whom I spend the bulk of my day simply do not struggle like the untold millions who wonder where their next meal will come from. Anyone compiling a list of "America's Least Wanted" would not turn to our congregation's membership directory for ideas.

The absence of disenfranchised people in our congregation, and in tens of thousands of others like ours, suggests an important responsibility. It suggests that we need to do a much better job of identifying in a more personal way with those who struggle. We need to find avenues to view underprivileged persons not as problems to be solved, but as people to join.

Something compels people of faith to try to *join* the poor. Something convinces us that we need to keep opening our lives to poorer persons, no matter how clumsy we are at the exercise. This "something" is, of course, the gospel. From start to finish, the message of holy scripture is that God gravitates toward people who dwell at the bottom of everyone else's priority list. The biblical bias for the poor and underprivileged is unmistakable.

To lift up but one example, the Bread for the World movement (www.bread.org) is an organized effort to get Americans to join their lives more closely with those for whom poverty jeopardizes every dream. It is a considerate effort built on the hope that supporters will take the circumstances of poorer people to heart. If you are unfamiliar with their work, Bread for the World goes after more than just friendly talk to allow those of us who live with means to feel good about our charitable thoughts. No, this organization advocates for particular legislation that benefits families in need and women, infants, and children who are not sure if anyone believes in them. Handing out money rarely answers systemic problems. Courageous legislation to change societal inequities is part of the solution. So if you have never signed on before to a legislative initiative, you might consider doing so as an active feature of your Christian life. A signature of yours on some worthy legislative petition, be it Bread for the World-endorsed or otherwise, might be that small act of love that enlarges your life and gives a reprieve to someone else's.

If advocating for the poor by way of signing a letter sounds too political for your spiritual sensibilities, try to remember the Lord's expectation that we have not only a personal faith but also an active faith. Here is something else to consider: If you were to look at the Hebrew word for "poor" (*'aniyyim*) alongside the word Hebrew word for "humble" (*'anawim*), there is very close spelling and relationship. The former is an economic state; the latter is a character condition. Poverty is a circumstance; humility is a choice. Yet both have in common one thing—non-possessiveness. Both poverty and humility are postures of people who are wide open to receiving the abundant grace of God.

Economic poverty may not be your lot. But if it isn't, see to it that humility figures credibly into your life. With humility deeply seated in our hearts, we can avoid a denigration of those who are poor, we can put aside condescending speech about those who struggle financially, and most pervasive of all, we can escape that inclination to ignore or dismiss those who live in poverty. Humility will school us in firsthand learning from those who struggle every day, and allow for more of God's grace to flow from them to us. It can free us from the personal hang-ups with comfort that tie up far too much of life. In our *humility,* we can discover a new kinship with others who live in *poverty*. Because according to Jesus, both the humble and the poor share the identity of being "blessed."

god's will

A horrific event happened in our community several years ago. A drunk driver—seriously drunk—went the wrong direction down an interstate ramp with his lights off. It was night on a rural section of Iowa Interstate. When his pick-up truck finally collided head-on with a lone car traveling at the same highway speed, there was no hope of survivors. He and the two high school girls in the car were killed instantly. The community grieved for days. People in all quarters were in anguish. I didn't know it was humanly possible to have a blood alcohol level of .256 and still function enough to drive.

The drunk driver was unknown to me. He was not a member of our congregation. But I performed his funeral as a favor to the family. That funeral ranks among the most difficult assignments I have ever undertaken. Only one dimension of that experience is pertinent to this page. A well-intentioned woman came up to me in the funeral home just prior to the service, saying, "Pastor, I can only imagine how difficult this is for you. And these poor families! Those poor girls! I'm sure God has a plan behind it all. We just don't know what it is." And then, raising slightly the pitch of her voice with a head tilt, she said, "Everything has a purpose, you know." I got mad. It was the angriest I have ever been at a funeral. This could not be left untouched. So, right then and there, fighting off the temptation to unload an expletive, I said, "Listen, here," grabbing her arm. "I don't know where you're coming from, but that is a bunch of baloney. I have no personal interest or belief in a God who would do this to people." I let it be at that and walked off to collect myself and get ready for the service. I know she deserved a whole lot more gentleness than I delivered that day.

There is a gross heresy at work throughout the Christian community. It involves the instinct to assign God responsibility for everything we cannot control or explain. God is said to arrange this and allow that. God causes all sorts of other things to happen for a purpose. When a fifty-five-foot-tall tower of logs collapsed in a Texas A & M bonfire of 1999, nineteen people were killed. Said one of the survivors: "It's a freak accident, that's all it is. God wanted it to happen, so it happened." This is called primitive theology. In the case of human suffering, it is blasphemous speech. Most suffering is meaningless. For every person who may grow spiritually as a result of suffering, plenty of others get the feathers kicked out of their faith by senseless tragedy.

To ascribe all events that we cannot control to "God's will" or "God's plan" is to trivialize both God and us. "It's not really true that I scratched my head; God made me scratch it!" If we have no independent faculties to make decisions and act with some autonomy, we are nothing but puppets. If God constantly overrules those faculties, then we live the life of a caged animal, never really free to let the Holy Spirit fly in us.

I am not suggesting that God lacks sovereignty. God is indeed sovereign. But the nature of divine sovereignty is not to exercise control over everything we do. God's awesome sovereignty is not diminished when God grants us the capability to make our own decisions and create many of our own circumstances. Biblically speaking, God cares a whole lot more about who we are than what we do. So God equips us with the inner resources we might need to deal with adversity and make wise and mature decisions. Every time we get preoccupied with God's will for determining our supermarket purchases or friendships, we confuse our own inverted pride with God's will. God becomes an ad hoc psychic advisor, a cosmic bellhop.

Did God have a purpose in mind for this inebriated man to climb into his pick-up truck and kill two girls? Not any Lord I can locate in scripture. Does God have endless compassion and empathy for all those suffering from this awful turn of events? Now we're talking Christ-sense.

fingertip control

When our twelve-year-old VCR malfunctioned a few years ago by refusing to rewind, fast forward, or even spit out the videotape, our young son Jacob announced disparagingly to his mother and father, in a phrase that's not easy to forget, "This is a really low-tech household." To this seventh grader, who had seen enough electronic paraphernalia in friends' homes to make him an expert on envy, Mom and Dad were from the Stone Age.

A trip to the electronics store with its dizzying noise and visual bombardment taught me two lessons. First, it is true, we have a fairly low-tech household. Second, we parents are not embarrassed by this fact. We *did* walk out with a $99 DVD player that, to my surprise, weighed the rough equivalent of a Big Mac hamburger. No more tapes chewed alive. In Jacob's book, this long-in-coming purchase probably ushered us right to the edge of a medium-tech household.

A new problem surfaced with that DVD player acquisition. Our family room table now had three remote control devices instead of two. To this day, no one including Jacob has mastered the use of all their features. More buttons reside on these contraptions than in the cockpit of a 757. If operating remote control gadgets presents a problem to fairly intelligent people, keeping track of them, I'm told, creates an even greater problem. A few years ago, Magnavox released a study indicating that more than half of all Americans lose their remote—sometimes called "the box"—between one and five times a week. In 63% of these search and rescue efforts, it took nearly five minutes to locate the device. Most people indicate they find the remote hiding in furniture or a nearby room; six percent say they usually find it in the refrigerator.

Who's to blame for this efflorescence of remote devices in the world and for their susceptibility to disappearance?

Gene Polley is his name. He's the Zenith engineer who in 1955 came up with the idea that we could be freed of the tyranny of ever having to move our behind off the couch. Properly speaking, we ought to call it by its full name: remote *control*. It is really all about control. Most every marriage or coupled relationship in the western world finds this device to be a bone of contention. Perfectly loving people fight over whose fingertips control life in the household. We maneuver our fingers and thumbs, blithely assuming that power in life is constituted by who controls the clicker, or the zapper, or *the box*.

But there is another way to put your fingertips to work. It's strikingly low-tech in comparison. Give it a try. Hold on to some flesh and blood if it has been a long time since you've held another person. Grasp the hand of someone you care about. Feel the incredible pulse of humanity. You don't have to be in love with this person. Just hold his or her hand and get in touch with really low-tech life. In the congregation I serve, we do this hand holding at the end of every church council meeting. We hold hands in a circle and pray. It may be the most important business our church conducts—which brings me to this thought about the mix of power and life.

The next time you find yourself grabbing the remote control away from someone else, or using your fingers to point in condemnation, or gesturing in such a way that presses down another human being, calmly tell yourself that there is no life in such illusions of power. There is only domination. How much more fruitful if we could learn from the example of a savior who once loosened his gnarled fingers enough to receive a couple of spikes. Power comes from letting go. That's the biblical message. Life comes from opening our hands to others. And from the hands of one nailed to the crossbar of a tree long ago, *life* has been emanating ever since.

anxious living

It is hard to agree on exactly what makes contemporary American life so different from times past. Romanticizing the past never does much for me. I start to yawn when a person rolls out predictable words like: "Everybody used to work hard. There were no slackers. Unshakable moral standards were honored. Litter didn't exist. Everybody prayed." We all know this is more nostalgia and wishful thinking than anything else.

There is one describable difference between past and present culture that seems fair to claim: in a pre-technological and more agrarian time, work was—generally speaking—more physically demanding and less anxiety producing. If the sheep needed shearing or the stove wood needed chopping or the hay needed bundling, one knew when the day's work was complete. In contrast, the complexity of modern life rarely allows us to know when things are actually done. Open-ended obligations keep rolling in. Extensive task lists accumulate. Our personal and professional lives merge. Countless external demands continually summon. Opportunities keep opening up.

Those who use e-mail know what I mean. E-mail never quits. I can check my inbox at midnight and clear away, reply to, or store all the unchecked messages that I left unattended earlier in the day. By 8:00 A.M., there are twenty new messages waiting to be read and dealt with, many from people living in other time zones. Our cell phones ring at any moment of the day. We get bleeping reminders of what we should be doing to meet a host of deadlines. You can plug the particulars of your life into any one of these sentences. The modern condition is to be *chronically anxious*, and often through no fault entirely of our own.

What makes contemporary anxiety so perplexing is a quirk of the human mind. We cannot quite remember all things. And yet, we cannot quite forget them either. Have you ever thought about this? Who among us can possibly remember everything we are supposed to do in a given week? Between job and personal life, friends and self, "shoulds" and "want-tos," there is no way to keep track without a calendar or notes of some kind. If you prize sanity or relationships, you cannot hold everything you are supposed to recall inside of your head.

By the same token, there is a perverse and mean trick of the brain by which we cannot completely forget things. Even when we keep a meticulous datebook, with everything imaginable in it, our brain keeps reminding us of things we have not done. It tells us of things we should have done. We suddenly recall promises we have not kept and people we said we'd "get back to." Most frustratingly, our minds alert us to these bothersome leftovers at *very* inopportune times—like in the middle of another conversation, or while driving in tense traffic, or at 2:00 A.M.

In the past, when this foible of the human brain awakened me at 2:00 A.M., I used to turn to a scrap of paper on the bedside table and write down some reminding words in the dark. What a joke that was! The chicken-scratch in the morning was illegible. Now what I usually do is grab my cell phone with its lighted keypad and dial my office voicemail. My wife loves to be jolted out of a deep dream in order to hear her husband whispering on a cell phone in the dark. "Who are you talking to?" she says in a panic. When I say "myself," she assumes it's all part of her dream and falls right back asleep.

Jesus gives us stirring words when he summons us to end anxious living (Matt. 6:25-34). It's a poetic sermon worth coming back to time and again. At the end of a long set of admonitions, his last pronouncement stands out for its candor: "Today's trouble is enough for today," he says (v. 34). The Lord is acknowledging that a substantial load of concern will fill every day. No exceptions. Anxiety-ridden realities are here to stay. The way we handle them is what will distinguish whether we really have a life—or not much of one at all.

faith rising from ashes

A thoughtful nineteen-year-old, full of spiritual quest and a lot of heart, stopped me as I was leaving his grandmother's funeral visitation. He asked me a probing question: "Pastor Marty, when did you get your faith?" Whoa! This was a big one. You don't just casually walk together toward your car, chew on a gritty funeral home mint, and address this mega question lightly. We sat down.

The tame reply would have had something to do with the day I was baptized. That would feel theologically correct. Lutheran Christians tend to think of God as something other than a gigantic fireworks display that converts the soul in one dramatic moment on one unforgettable day. More like dust mites that won't leave your house alone, God works under the radar—quietly, invisibly, and with incredible constancy, always in the hope of gaining *at least* one chamber of our heart.

This strapping nineteen-year-old wasn't after a tame reply. He wanted the real deal. So I told him about that day in my life that *was* different. It is the day faith came off the page and became a living reality. Never again would I wrestle with faith as an abstraction. In July 1982, I drove over to the neighborhood church where our family had planted itself for the prior two decades. Fresh home from a year and a half in Africa, it was my task to pick up the urn containing my mother's ashes. It seemed like a fair assignment. Several brothers and Dad had done yeomen's work the previous year, caring lovingly for Mother when I was away. Cancer had withered her once athletic body into exhaustion and death. Resurrection was the only thing that could make good on the idiocy of such a ravaging disease.

Pastor led me to the basement of the church. As we descended the steps, he spoke all sorts of grace-filled words about what this woman named Elsa meant to him, to that congregation, and to the world. I loved my mother and admire this pastor, both still so deeply. He unlocked the church vault. Then, quite unceremoniously, he placed the canister containing Mother's cremains—that would be her ashes—into my hands. The light steel urn was nothing fancy. The non-descript label on top had Mother's name and dates of birth and death.

Pastor and I exchanged an embrace before I headed out into the summer sun to load the urn into the trunk of the family Mustang. I pulled out slowly, so as not to tip the urn, and began the long and lonely drive to northern Wisconsin. There we would hold a brief service and bury Mother's cremains on a windy day in the country cemetery.

Two thoughts kept colliding in my head as I drove. First, there were the questions I posed to myself: What happens if I get in an accident? Should I have put the urn on the floor next to me instead of in the trunk? Which would signal greater reverence? What if I get rear-ended? How is it that a woman who almost beat me in an arm-wrestling challenge *before* Africa, can now be reduced to a small paint can *after* Africa? Second, though, there were words of an apostle named Paul that kept getting into my head. "If Christ was not raised from the dead, everything you call faith is futile, Peter. Everything you are up to is a waste of time. You can believe whatever you want and be spooked by whatever you wish, including those ashes in the trunk. But I'm telling you, Christ was raised from the dead so that you and yours can be also."

The searching questions I had been rolling around like dice in my head were strangely silenced on that drive. It was the eloquence of Paul. Yes, it was. Faith came alive that day as I steered the Mustang through lush Wisconsin farm fields, one after another. I cannot say exactly how it all happened. But the same faith that came alive that day has held me ever since.

weightless grace

weightless grace

the hawaiian man

Two weeks ago my plane landed after midnight at Los Angeles International airport. This was a 24-hour over-and-back deal, just enough time to attend a portion of the National Religious Broadcasters Convention. At the crowded underground pick-up curb, I waved down Blue Super Shuttle no. 859. A large man in a Hawaiian shirt, who could have doubled as a waiter for some Indonesian island beach café, disappeared with my bag behind the rear tailgate. I climbed into this Ford Econoline van (where I hoped my bag was loaded), dragging my body uncomfortably over several other bodies. This is the peculiar behavior in which one engages when angling for the one available seat at the rear of a stretch van. It was pitch dark. I counted five heads in front of me.

The Hawaiian Man got behind the wheel and off we went. What possesses one to press the gas pedal all the way to the floor and swerve between six lanes of virtually grid-locked ground transportation traffic, when all of the cars and vans just seventy-five feet ahead are at a standstill, I'll never know. I think it has something to do with intimidating others from trying to beat you to a merge. Come at the driver's door of another taxi with enough speed to threaten his life, and he'll back off. The Hawaiian Man had a master's degree, I determined, in aggressive instinct with brake and accelerator. How else could he repeatedly pull off the same trick every hundred yards? I quickly realized I was trusting the entirety of my life to this guy in a snazzy blue shirt.

I reached for the six-foot-long seatbelt dangling from the ceiling. It hung there helplessly, an obvious sign that the retraction spring had broken or jammed. I buckled into it anyway, partly out of habit and partly so that a medic scraping me off a median wall might notice my strong desire to live.

It was Grammy Awards night in L.A. At 1:00 A.M. the eight-lane freeway traffic was thick. I said hello to the other shadows in the van. Nobody answered. Something gave me the distinct impression that every one of them spoke a different language than I did. We hurtled along in the dark on I-5. The Hawaiian Man kept fiddling with his keyboard on the dash, punching in odd numbers and letters that meant nothing to me at all. Every time he turned to read the LED, we swerved. I sat up tall enough to see how fast we were going in the carpool lane. It was just below ninety miles per hour, give or take "one." There were innocent people in this van. I was one of them.

I distracted myself from this L.A. freeway madness by practicing my pronunciation of the highway exit signs: Carmenita. Rostrata. Caballero. La Palma. The rear seat in a stretch van, if you've never had the experience, offers a primer in pothole and road bump detail while making a milk shake of one's stomach. Would that I had something in my stomach besides six pretzels from the airline "meal." A milk shake sounded pretty good.

Here's the strangest part of all: I not only trusted my life to The Hawaiian Man; I actually paid him for the experience! Still crazier, I *tipped* him, which I now consider not remuneration for good service, but a gift of gratitude for allowing me to step out alive at the Anaheim hotel. As I stumbled with my suitcase to the counter of the night clerk, one thought kept coming to my sleepy head. I said to myself, "If I can trust everything I am and care about to The Hawaiian Man, who plays so lightly and easily with my life, how much more can I trust myself to the Lord who doesn't play lightly with me at all." I knew the answer. I went to my room and slept like a baby.

legato

Most weeks of the year, I spend a day commuting across Illinois between a Chicago radio studio and a Davenport, Iowa, Lutheran Church. I fuel up the car with gas, fuel up my head with caffeine, and off I go. The scenery is expansive farmland, flat but lush fields of rich soil. Red-tailed hawks sit atop the highway signs looking for their next meal. When the radio stations fade, and I get tired of the same old CDs playing in the changer, I look for other entertainment. Each week, without fail, it's always there, right overhead. What a stunning sight!

Starlings flying in formation create an avian air show second to none. These tiny birds flock together by the hundreds—or is it thousands?—and then swoop, dip, and climb in perfect unison. It's one of the most fascinating phenomena in nature. I get so wrapped up watching their maneuvers that I have to remember to glance occasionally at the road. They roll through the sky like a big magic carpet gently rippling in the wind. They ride the currents with a seamless unity in the most carefree of ways.

I heard a Brahms violin concerto at the symphony the other night. It was the sort of musical feast I thought was reserved for heaven. How little I must know about heaven, or heaven on earth. The artist's legato playing with full bow was absolutely transcendent. I'll never know how one can manage to play so effortlessly. The smoothness. The musicality. The lyrical glide. He took every young struggling violinist in the audience on a ride they will not soon forget.

Illinois starlings fly legato. I can't speak for Nebraska starlings or Pennsylvania starlings. But the Illinois bunch have it down. They intuit Brahms. Their perfect synchronicity has a smoothness that nothing else in aerial creation quite replicates. Like willow branches swaying in a breeze, or a gifted violinist floating through complex movements, these starlings have a coordinated fluency to their flight. Call it *legato*. Their wings may beat twenty-five times a second, but to the naked eye they are enjoying the most graceful roller coaster ride ever invented.

We wonder how these flocks stick together and dip and dive so uniformly. How is that they can be so together in one instant, explode into an indecipherable mess the next, and suddenly re-gather a second later? This change-up occurs whenever a predatory bird shows up and threatens the flock. From an outside perspective, it would seem that one lead starling must be masterminding this disperse-and-reassemble action. But not so. There is no agreed-upon strategy. There is no chieftain at the head of the pack. It is simply a matter of each starling following three basic rules: (1) stay two or three body lengths away from your neighbor; (2) do not collide with any other starling; and (3) dive fast if a hawk shows up. These rules keep a flock moving and headed in the same direction.

Christian congregations that know how to move with spontaneity, and yet with order inside that spontaneity, are what I call *legato congregations*. They don't obsess over rules, yet they have them. They don't have a hierarchical plan for every new initiative, yet things get done. Through the smooth interplay of people trying to find their way together, legato congregations move purposefully through life.

The writer of Acts describes the first example of this kind of community, flourishing as it did from the spontaneous order that comes when people are spiritually in synch with one another. According to Acts 4, these early believers experienced a palpable unity with one another—"those who believed were of one heart and soul" (v. 32). They practiced sharing their possessions—"everything they owned was held in common"(v. 32). Every individual in the community had the basic necessities of life covered—"there was not a needy person among them"(v. 34). The power of their resurrection testimony provided them with an aroma of grace—"great grace was upon them all"(v. 33).

Oh, the grace of legato—high above in a flock of birds or far below in a group of believers.

life in the pew

Monday morning at our church is a fascinating time. That's when clean-up volunteers discover what the youth group did the night before. It's when the receptionist pitches the remaining donuts, now petrified, that were never disposed of the day before. Monday morning is when the custodians survey the wreckage and make their to-do lists for the week. As they make rounds they encounter the bizarre, the funny, and sometimes the disgusting. It's a good thing there are some surprises mixed in with the mundane tasks. Otherwise our crew might lose their sense of humor and love for the congregation.

In a recent Monday pew cleaning operation, Matt came across a Sunday leftover. It was a little piece of scratch paper from the envelope slot stuck to the back of the pew. On it were scrawled four imperatives: 1. Stop folding paper. 2. Sit down. 3. Pay attention. 4. Sing #508. At the bottom were more handwritten words, a few of them underlined: "You are <u>really</u> <u>close</u> to <u>no</u> <u>Burger</u> <u>King</u>!"

On first read I guessed this to be a parent scolding a child. But that could be presumptuous. Who is to say it wasn't from the hand of some woman trying to get her husband to pay attention during worship. I can picture him fumbling around with receipts and old papers in his front pockets, repeatedly standing up to get the crumpled sheets out, while she glares at him. "No Burger King brunch for you, buddy, unless you sit down and sing."

Or maybe it was some father hoping his fifteen-year-old will start glowing a bit more brightly in worship and let the Holy Spirit grab hold of his frown. "Come on, Brian. Sing #508 like you mean it."

"But, Dad, I'm not into singing this morning."

"Fine, son. Then there's no Whopper and fries for you. You'll be eatin' peanut butter and jelly in your room."

I rely on my wife Susan for descriptions of what life in the pew is really like. Without her, I'd have little sense of the true pulse of life in the trenches. By the nature of pastoral ministry, I have sat beside my own children in worship relatively few times in their life. So, I have always counted on Susan to inform me of the love that transpires, the praises that get sung, the quiet battles that get waged, and the thousands of little communications that happen between family members.

Some Sundays over the years, she'd report that the kids were magnificent. They sang every hymn. They participated with gusto. They looked after each other in the kindest of ways. They truly loved the whole idea of being in church with God. Other weeks weren't nearly so smooth. It was the next thing to hand-to-hand combat. They were not "into it" at all on those Sundays. Of course, we adults have our days too. We just disguise our "not into it" moments a little better. Every young family has their humorous moments too. Nobody can find the right page. The second grader sings the wrong verse of a hymn. One child turns the page too quickly when she and Mom are sharing the same hymnal. Dad mispronounces a word, only to have his son look over with an eye roll.

This pew behavior is all part of the joy of coming together to praise the Lord. To be sure, life in the pew has its quirks and idiosyncrasies, but it also has its graces. In their best moments people are quick to look out for one another. They enjoy the privilege of worshiping together. When hospitality hums, no one sits alone, especially not the lonely, the grieving, or the guest. The warmth of Christian fellowship and the beauty of congregational love become very tangible in those moments. Through it all, God must delight in our weekly effort to put on the brakes of life and give thanks, surely cracking a smile on those days when the threat of "No Burger King for lunch" hangs heavy in the air.

on boredom

Scripture tells us the world would be a far better place if each of us did our part to live with a bit more godliness. If only we would tune in more regularly to the depths of who God made us to be, all kinds of things might flourish.

Question: How on earth do we tune in more sharply to who God made us to be without becoming hopelessly self-preoccupied or suddenly reliant on some flaky self-help book?

Answer: Sit in a room all by oneself.

That's the word from Anthony Bloom, the late archbishop of the Russian Orthodox Church. Bloom has done some interesting things in his life, including earlier work as a hospital surgeon for the French during WWII. But back to his suggestion for sitting in a room: "Try to find time to stay alone with yourself. Shut the door and settle down in your room at a moment when you have nothing else to do. Say, 'I am now with myself,' and just sit with yourself. After an amazingly short time you will most likely feel bored. This teaches us one very useful thing. It gives us insight into the fact that if after ten minutes of being alone with ourselves we feel like that, it is no wonder that others should feel equally bored [with us]."[25]

We all ought to give Bloom's experiment an honest try. Before you say you could not survive ten minutes in an empty room, just remember that hostages in deprived settings do it every day, all day. So, you can certainly manage some time in solitude if you put your mind to it.

I've never read a book on boredom. I don't know of any college or university that offers a course on boredom, though I had one professor whose teaching style acquainted me with the sensation. It is a complex phenomenon, the fear of which causes us to do some strange things. Take, for example, a woman who now shares toothpaste and whole lot else with a new man. She did not wake up one morning and say, "Oh, it's a perfect day to commit adultery." No, she simply woke up to another day where nothing much seemed to be happening in her marriage and the attention of another man became the perfect remedy for her boredom. Or take a man who loves to exaggerate his accomplishments. His pattern of embellishment probably has less to do with a desire for recognition and more to do with ending the personal boredom over the monotony of his days.

The fear of boredom causes all of us to do some outrageous things. I wonder, though, if we'd do as many of these things if we were more in tune with the high hopes of what God asks us to be. Sure, we could turn life into a constant quest for innovative alternatives—leapfrogging jobs, spouses, friends, and surroundings whenever life became dull. But that would get old. The quest itself would become a full-time occupation.

Perhaps we have grown accustomed to boredom because we have been so steeped in the idea that life is mostly entertainment. When something no longer titillates, we move easily into the zone of boredom. The great preacher Fred Craddock remarked one time on our quest for amusement. "Passengers on cruise ships, after nine beautiful sunsets and eighty-six invigorating games of shuffleboard, begin to ask the crew hopefully, 'Do you think we will have a storm?'"[26]

There is no magic to discovering meaning to life that is deeper than entertainment. All kinds of methods can get you there. But Anthony Bloom may be on to something. Find yourself a chair and an empty room. Sit patiently. Deal with yourself. Spend as much time as it takes, even realizing what other people have to live with in you. If you can sustain this discipline for any period of time without getting too bored with yourself, WOW! Get ready to receive God in a brand new way. God will be right there for you.

two passports

Writer Susan Sontag had a bout with cancer in the late 1970s. When later reflecting on her treatment and hospitalization, she wrote these memorable words: "Illness is the night-side of life, a more onerous citizenship. Everyone who is born holds dual citizenship, in the kingdom of the well and in the kingdom of the sick. Although we all prefer to use only the good passport, sooner or later each of us is obliged, at least for a spell, to identify ourselves as citizens of that other place."[27]

When I turned forty years old, I was obliged to pull out my second passport. I had glanced at it before. A stubbed toe, a broken finger, malaria at one time—these were all inconveniences in my past. But this time, I actually had to display my second passport and identify myself as a true citizen in the kingdom of the sick. Debilitating nerve pain in my arms resulted in a laminectomy, a surgical procedure on two vertebrae in my neck. Lying in a hospital bed told me that I was less a patient than a marginally cooperative *im*patient. I tried to use the time to let go of the busyness in my mind and learn more about grace. It wasn't easy. But these are among the things I noticed in that laboratory of grace:

The ceiling: I counted tiny pin holes patterned into the ceiling panels above my bed. There were forty-nine squares on every panel, with forty-nine pinholes in each, making for a grand total of 2,401 holes per panel.

Hospital gowns: These tie-in-the-back deals remain the only article of clothing in the world where one size fits all. Like modern health insurance, my gown kept reminding me that every time one turns around there is something else lacking coverage.

Television: If there be any doubt why Americans have such feeble attention spans, it clearly relates to television.

Flipping the clicker between sixty-nine channels only made me hungrier for human conversation and for that bag of magazines from home to arrive.

Nurses: The profession of nursing remains, I am quite sure, among the more quietly heroic professions around. What magnificent men and women these are who dedicate themselves to often very thankless tasks.

Oral swabs: Those little green sponge contraptions—fake lollipops—that allow you to "taste" cold water in the hours after surgery are as terrific as they're cracked up to be.

Josephine: I can only hope she is doing better now. She was the patient in the neighboring room who continuously shouted, "Help!" from 11:15 P.M. until 4:45 A.M. A nurse checked in on her no less than every five minutes.

Suffering: Almost every patient can say with integrity, "There are a lot of people suffering worse than I am." Not enough patients can say happily, "I belong to a congregation that loves God and cares for me."

Jesus: An eight-inch-tall crucifix of a triumphant Christ with arms upraised was mounted high on the wall. It was my twenty-four-hour-a-day sign of the Lord's presence. Except for the TV, Jesus was the only thing I could see without my bed tipped up. A sheetrock screw, gruesomely drilled beneath the chin of Jesus, made sure this Christ could not be stolen.

Surgeons: They do remarkable things. No doubt about it. Still, I wonder what their work would add up to were it not for the larger mystery of healing where God coagulates the serum, sends fiberblasts out across the skin edges, and has those fiberblasts make collagen. Watching a wound heal over the course of time can be a spiritual experience.

I put my second passport away a few weeks later but only after having learned new ways that illness teaches. Beyond the technical skill of hospital personnel, there were the human kindnesses too many to count. Gentle gestures of comfort and conversation make all the difference in the world when you're feeling lousy. They are like nuggets of grace that tip the scale from the weight of discouragement to the weightlessness of hope—and send us on our way.

december gentleness

Squirrel pie is a delicacy I have no intention of tasting. When a member of our congregation tried to talk me into it after a recent squirrel hunt, it was easy to say, "No thanks." The dish has zero appeal for me. I must have missed that day in science class a long time ago when the teacher said that there actually *are* modern people who choose to eat rodents when they certainly would not have to for survival. Adding to my present discomfort are lingering shivers from childhood when squirrels would get trapped in the attic rafters above my bed. However rational or irrational, my bias against these gnawing creatures of the rodent family, *Sciuridae,* is long-standing. Why would anyone take a three-day hunting trip into Iowa's backwoods to shoot a ball of fur, when they could have a field day in my own backyard? I'll never understand.

For most of the past year, our family of four has been united in its opinion of squirrels. These are the scrappy creatures who keep attacking our bird feeder, stealing what they can from the finches and cardinals who regularly drop in. Over the months, however, our unity has eroded. In recent days, I have found myself all alone. My wife Susan led the charge of empathy for the squirrels. One day she simply stopped opening the sliding door with the "chase instinct" and put the broomstick down. "They need to eat too," she chided. Our children, Jacob and Rachel, stood in solidarity with me for many months, startling the critters by shouting and screaming. We all believed our verbal nastiness might have some lasting repellant power. I redesigned the elaborate hanging device for the bird feeder every time a squirrel knocked it down. My efforts only encouraged them more. The day I smeared petroleum jelly up and down the feeder post made for a slip-and-slide show I'll never forget. It also tested our marriage in a fresh way.

Recently, the squirrels have gone straight for the warehouse. When they began gnawing on the five-gallon bucket lid of Wagner's wild bird seed outside, the kids and I marshaled new alarm. For a brief moment, I thought Susan was realigning with the forces of moral correctness when she said confidently, "They'll never get in there." Yesterday, she was out patiently sweeping up the plastic shards of the bucket lid as a squirrel feasted on the food remnants spilled across the deck.

These days, Jacob and Rachel no longer pound the glass door with their knuckles. Now they whisper in reverential tones from the kitchen table, concerned that several more decibels might scare their furry friends from the bucket feast. Now, what was there left for me to do? Recognizing that I might be the next one attacked with a broomstick, I decided early today (not yet publicly announced) that my assault on the squirrels is over.

What exactly happened to foster the change? Why this softening over time? Obviously, something in all of us eased up over the months. We all gave up trying to tame these squirrels and have them behave in our preferred way. I don't know all the reasons for our family alliance collapsing, but it has something to do with understanding that comes with the passage of time. It has something to do with the onset of a wintry landscape outside and honest empathy for creatures who have to work to find food. If the ancient Israelites could let their fields lie fallow every so many years for the poor to come in and feast (Exod. 23:11), our little family could certainly afford to let squirrels lay siege to a bucket. Eventually we came to the realization that it is not worth trying to manage what is beyond our control. Something akin to a voice from nowhere, yet deep inside, kept saying to me these many weeks, "Peter, you cannot tame what was never meant to be tamed. Wildness is wildness. But you know there is something else. Generosity is also generosity. Let both be prized by you." And so I learned about wildness and generosity this year—just a bit more slowly than some others around me.

ownership crisis

Considering the fact the Jesus borrowed virtually everything he ever used, it is a bit peculiar that we who follow him have such a strong impulse to own things. Jesus borrowed his meal sites, his nautical pulpits, and his different residences. He even borrowed the tomb at the end of his life. So, what's with our obsession with ownership? What brings us, at least on occasion, to say, "This is *my* life to live as I want," and, "It's *my* time to do with as I please"? That love of the word *my* has something to do with our desire to control circumstances and environment. We are creatures who behave with a dangerous sense of entitlement.

Dennis Hope is an interesting fellow, in case you haven't heard or read of him. He is the man who has been selling people property on the moon for more than twenty-five years. This is not a joke. It all began after a divorce in 1980 when Hope found himself low on cash. Looking up at the moon one night he thought to himself, "Now there's a lot of property up there." He began to research who owned the moon. The United Nations' Outer Space Treaty of 1967 forbids any government from owning planetary property, but it does not specifically say individuals cannot own land in outer space. Dennis Hope went to work. Nobody stopped him. He filed a claim at a San Francisco courthouse. He then divided up the moon's estimated ten billion acres of land into small individual parcels.

Anyone who sends in money can receive a certificate of deed with the precise coordinates of their property printed on it. Hope has now shrunk the lot sizes to one acre each and raised the price to $19.99. His company, Lunar Embassy, has sold more than 430 million acres on the moon, totaling more than $6.5 million. What, you may ask, drives thousands of people to purchase real estate on the moon, when this magnificent orb is theirs to look at every night? Well, it's called ownership. The idea that we must own practically everything, including many things that were never meant to be personal property, infatuates us.

C. S. Lewis writes in his satirical work, *The Screwtape Letters,* about our use of the little word *my*. Too many of us, he says, are like the spoiled child who thinks that "my teddy bear" means it is mine to destroy. In reality, "my teddy bear" is an indication that that teddy bear exists to comfort me and be my friend. Insecurity, and its corollary control, can give us weird ideas of domination. We live in God's world, yet we behave as if it is "my world" to do with as I please. My wife is a treasure in her own right who cannot be possessed. Yet, C. S. Lewis reminds us, we can easily treat a spouse as a possession at our disposal.[28]

One day Jesus told a painful parable about some wicked tenants who leased vineyard property from an owner (Matt. 21:33-44). When harvest came and the owner sent his slaves to collect the produce, the tenants systematically beat up those slaves. Figuring that the tenants would respect his son, the owner sent that son to reason with the tenants, only to find they killed him. As far as the tenants were concerned, this son was the only obstacle standing in the way of what they would inherit. It's a tragic parable about confusing a lease arrangement with ownership, borrowing with possessing.

St. Benedict was adamant that monks in his order would hold all property in common. The private ownership of something as small as a pencil was prohibited without special permission of the Abbot. It wasn't the material object itself that posed the danger, reasoned Benedict. It was the appropriation of that object as a personal possession that led to spiritual trouble.

Benedictine monks aren't the only ones ready to question our love affair with the words *my* and *mine*. So are all who profess Christ and who notice his penchant for borrowing.

chilean sea bass

A friend and I settled into lunch at a nice Italian restaurant the other day. His eyes went right to Chilean sea bass on the menu. I said, "You know, John, Chilean sea bass is a made-up name for marketing a trash fish. It really is. I just read about it last week—the marketing strategy that turns undesirable fish into palatable new commodities for restaurants." It wasn't the most brilliantly timed remark on my part. It would have been better to say nothing at all. John thanked me kindly for my warm introduction to a tasty meal conversation. He then ordered a cashew chicken spinach salad.

It is true. Chilean sea bass is a concocted name for what is really the Patagonian toothfish. It isn't bass at all. And, it's only found peripherally in Chilean seas. Until a host of other fish populations became decimated by human consumption, the Patagonian toothfish was of virtually no interest to anyone but elephant seals. Now it's on the menu of elegant restaurants. The same marketing company that gave the kiwi name to Chinese gooseberries also came up with the Chilean sea bass moniker. Orange roughy, you may not want to know if you're a fish lover, is really the marketed name for a trash fish called slimehead.

What's in a name? Well, evidently a lot of emotion and symbolism. Canadian authorities sent Ottawa residents into an uproar some years ago when they banned the Central Experimental Farm there from using human names for cows. Some feared that a child named Elsie, for example, might be embarrassed to meet a cow with the same name. Or, a woman finding her name on a cow that she deemed to be old and ugly might suffer serious emotional stress. By the way, Clover and Buttercup made the exemption list of approved names. What's in a name? There is more power than we often realize. A name communicates essence and significance. Speak someone's name and you reveal a personality, a history, indeed a whole world of meaning.

When Moses saw a bush enflamed before his eyes one day, he wanted to know one thing above all else. Who was this behind the smoke, and what name did this one bear besides the puzzling, "I am who I am"? If you can brand someone with a name, you have a chance of feeling that person's presence every time it gets uttered. That's because a name is more than a label or an arbitrary designation. It's a way of articulating some identity. When the angel Gabriel tells an astonished Joseph that he should name his boy Jesus, "for he will save his people from their sins," Gabriel is suggesting a name with a purpose. *Jesus*, meaning "God saves," is to be the very embodiment of what the Lord does for a living.

Recently, I struck up a conversation with a young boy in our congregation. He was all enthused about his Sunday school class. Probing his happiness further, I asked him, "Who is your teacher?" He told me he didn't know. I grew sad. Sunday school had been in session for four months running, and I could tell this boy loved his teacher. "You really don't know her name?" I asked, a bit befuddled. "No," he said, "she never told us." My guess is that the woman probably did tell her class but in too quick of a way that never got repeated, at least not enough times for a second grader.

My private guess is that many of us could afford to share our own name more generously with those whom we meet, whether we teach kids in a church or not. Sharing one's name is pretty indispensable to honest hospitality. As simple as it is, it's fundamental to orienting another person gracefully. It's how we give people a foothold on who we are. A name is the stuff of identity. So, presuming that no one would ever *think* of naming a cow after you once they hear your name, what have you got to lose? Let people in on your name. You will be giving them valuable access to some of your beautiful significance.

hold the fries

When I quit my French fry consumption six years ago, I quit cold turkey. It happened while staring down the cooking oil troughs in a fast food joint one day. I watched a high school kid haul the fries from the sizzling oil to the heat lamps, and my imagination went berserk. I began to picture individual fries getting lodged completely whole into two-inch sections of the central arteries exiting my heart. It wasn't rational, mind you, but imagination rarely is. Once I had my own vivid image of what this tasty food was doing to my cardio-vascular health, that was it. No more inhaling what I had come to savor so thoroughly.

My own abstinence hasn't dented the potato market. In 1960 Americans consumed an average of four pounds of frozen French fries. Forty years later that average had risen to thirty pounds per year. People are nuts about these Russett Burbank potatoes peeled and cut into strips. Well, most people are crazy about them. Some of us have this artery obsession issue I mentioned. Others, I've come to find out, have a religious problem with fries.

Rev. Massimo Salani of Tuscany, Italy, tops the list of religious naysayers. He is the Catholic priest who catapulted into international fame a few years ago when he railed against the influx of fast food restaurants in his country. Until recently, Italians have been known for their three-hour lunch. Salani's claim that French fries, hamburgers, and Coke are good for nothing is what brought a storm of protest his way. He wrote a controversial piece about fast food being fit for Protestants but not for Catholics. Martin Luther, he suggested, was responsible for introducing an individualized faith to Christianity, something Salani connects with the modern fetish for fast food. The Catholic Church, he reasoned, has a strong communitarian understanding that naturally resists this eat-and-run dining mentality. Writing about food is unquestionably this man's passion. Delivering indigestion to others is largely the result. He has criticized Catholics for eating too much and Muslims for not having "a balanced diet." Now it's Protestants and French fries getting sizzled in oil and baked under a heat lamp.

It's too bad Martin Luther isn't around to drop in on Father Salani, split a Big Mac, and clarify a few things. Luther had a strong doctrine of the church and a deep sense of Christian community. Few theologians would characterize the reformer's thinking as individualistically-minded. After all, this was the professor who invited students over for supper around the family table and whose students published volumes of Table Talk to recount those communal moments.

The Slow Food movement in Italy—there actually is such a movement worldwide—is not completely ready to embrace Salini's ideas. Giacomo Mojoli, vice president of the Slow Food organization, refuses to give wholehearted approval to the priest's ways. "Fast foods are dangerous because they bring about the homogenization of taste," he said. "But there is no sense in demonizing them."[29]

If I could meet Massimo Salini, I would ask him what he thinks of the ancient Israelites eating manna in the wilderness. As far as I can tell, that manna feast in Exodus 16 is a biblical treatise on fast food. Remember how rapidly those complaining Israelites had to eat the flaky stuff? If they waited too long, the sun of the day would cause it to vanish. If they tried to keep it in Tupperware for the night, worms would have it fouled up by dawn. The Lord told the people that they had no choice but to consume manna fast. What would Father Salini have done had he been among those itinerant people? I'll have to ask him when we sit down for a meal. It may take us awhile to agree on how fast or slow to eat together. But I know we'll share one thing in common: neither one of us will order fries.

growing new

I use the phrase "growing old" as frequently as everyone else does. It's a quick way to refer to the aging process that touches the bodies and minds of all of us. When I'm thinking well and fast on my feet, sometimes I will use the more politically correct expression, "Growing old*er*," which is supposed to sound less terminal.

Either way, both expressions have their problems. It's not that we should shrink from facing old age with a lot of candor and grace. The last thing we need in a culture where perpetual youth is elevated to a god is to consider old age a problem. My issue isn't with the word *old* or *older;* it's connecting the word *growing* with it. The little green plant beside my desk adds newness to itself each day. There are new roots, new branches, new leaves, and new blossoms. Well, there aren't new blossoms and new leaves *every* day. But you know what I mean. They are in the process of becoming, even when my naked eye cannot see them.

Growth is about adding something new. That's why "growing old" is a contradiction in terms. How can you *grow* old? You can only grow new, which is what growth means in the first place. I am always invigorated by the stories of people who catch this idea of growing new. Some of them I meet in living color as I watch older volunteers do courageous and interesting things with their days. Some of them I experience vicariously. Here is one I have only read about.

A ninety-one-year-old great-grandmother has been hired by a Norwegian bar owner to be its bouncer. Stavanger is a western coastal city about 185 miles from the capital, Oslo. Police in that community have imposed a new rule that all bars and pubs must have a bouncer on weekends to prevent trouble. Marta Aurenes is familiar with the digs she is now guarding. Since turning eighty-six she has been a regular patron of the bar. "I can be pretty strict if I have to be," she said upon signing on. Although Aurenes doesn't expect any trouble, she has—catch this!—been working out with weights three times a week.

Norwegians have always evoked an image of sturdiness. But who knew they were this tough?

So what do we do with persons who think that life is all downhill after the age of &#@%? What do we do with those who are determined to believe that aging means that each day you can only do less, look worse, and get more of life drained out of you? We could send them to Stavanger, Norway, for a drink, or for a bench-pressing session with Marta. Or we could help them relax into the grace of growing new.

The Bible doesn't offer any help on the problem of old age because in the Bible old age isn't considered a problem. It is a blessing. To die "full of years" is one of the greatest gifts of God. Near the end of the Old Testament there is a wonderful image of what Jerusalem will look like once restored: "Old men and old women shall again sit in the streets of Jerusalem, each with a staff in hand because of their great age. And the streets of the city shall be full of boys and girls playing" (Zech. 8:4-5). We're obviously not living in the new Jerusalem yet. Our first clue of its arrival will be when we start constructing more preschools inside nursing home complexes and retirement centers. The effort has begun, but not many commercial real estate developers or builders are catching on. Maybe we need to give them free Bibles with sticky notes marking Zechariah's eighth chapter. Or, I suppose we could just wait patiently for the new Jerusalem, drawing inspiration from all the ninety-one-year-olds out there who are *growing new*, each in his or her own way, cane in hand or not.

notes

1. Stuart Feder, *Charles Ives, My Father's Song: A Psychoanalytic Biography* (New Haven: Yale University Press, 1992), 101.

2. Peter Smith, *Onward!: 25 Years of Advice, Exhortation, and Inspiration from America's Best Commencement Speeches* (New York: Simon and Schuster, 2000), 55.

3. C. S. Lewis, *The Screwtape Letters* (New York: HarperCollins, 2001), 60.

4. Ibid., 61.

5. Timothy George, *John Robinson and the English Separatist Movement* (Macon, Ga.: Mercer University Press, 1982), 1.

6. Philip Yancey, *Reaching for the Invisible God* (Grand Rapids: Zondervan, 2000), 202.

7. Elie Wiesel, "The Perils of Indifference" (speech presented at the White House as part of the Millennium Lecture series, Washington, D.C., April 12, 1999).

8. Yancey, *Reaching for the Invisible God,* 201.

9. Barbara Brown Taylor, *Speaking of Sin* (Cambridge, Mass.: Cowley Publications, 2001), 86.

10. James Cowan, *Desert Father: A Journey in the Wilderness with Saint Anthony* (Boston: Shambhala, 2004), 105.

Sebastian Bock, *The "Egg" of the Pala Montefeltro by Piero della Francesca and its Symbolic Meaning* (Heidelberg, 2002), 6, 17–21.

11. Ben Witherington III, *Incandescence: Light Shed by the Word* (Grand Rapids: Eerdmanns, 2006), 112.

12. Leo Tolstoy, *Confession,* trans. David Patterson (New York: W.W. Norton & Company, 1996), 34.

13. Madeleine L'Engle, *Glimpses of Grace: Daily Thoughts and Reflections* (San Francisco: HarperSanFrancisco, 1998), 121.

14. Jimmy Carter and Boutros Boutros-Ghali, "Conference for Global Development Cooperation." *Conference Report Series* 4, no. 2 (2000): 9.

15. Jimmy Carter, "What Makes a Person's Life Worthwhile," *Family Circle Magazine*, January 5, 1999, 112.

16. Dietrich Bonhoeffer, *Dietrich Bonhoeffer: Witness to Jesus Christ* (Minneapolis: Fortress Press, 1991), 183.

17. Emily Thornton, "What the Amazing Japanese Are Up to Now," *Fortune*, June 29, 1992.

18. Thomas J. McSweeney and Stephanie Raha, *Better to Light One Candle* (New York: Continuum International, 1999), 11.

19. Tad Friend, "Jumpers," *The New Yorker*, October 13, 2003.

20. Meredith Stoffel, "Prank Backfires, Man Swallows Key," The Odd Truth, *CBSnews.com*, June 27, 2005, http://www.cbsnews.com/stories/2005/06/28/national/main704832.shtml?source=searchstory (accessed June 23, 2008).

21. Madeleine L'Engle, *Glimpses of Grace: Daily Thoughts and Reflections* (San Francisco: HarperSanFrancisco, 1998), 66.

22. See Steven Pivovar, "Ambidextrous Pitcher Could Move Up To Next Level," *Omaha World-Herald,* April 24, 2007, or Alan Schwarz, "Throwing Batters Curves Before Throwing a Pitch," *New York Times,* April 6, 2007.

23. "Backwards driver's peace mission," *BBC News*, February 19, 2004, http://news.bbc.co.uk/2/hi/south_asia/3503651.stm (accessed June 23, 2008).

24. "To Sleep, Perchance to Hear," *Johns Hopkins Magazine,* June 1998.

25. Anthony Bloom, *Beginning To Pray* (Mahwah, N.J.: Paulist, 1982), 67–68.

26. Fred B. Craddock, *Overhearing the Gospel* (Atlanta: Chalice, 2002), 6.

27. Susan Sontag, *Illness as Metaphor and AIDS and Its Metaphors* (New York: PicadorUSA, 2001), 3.

28. C. S. Lewis, *The Complete C. S. Lewis Signature Classics* (San Francisco: HarperSanFrancisco, 2002), 168.

29. "Priest excommunicates fast food," *Amarillo Globe News,* December 7, 2000, http://www.amarillo.com/stories/120700/bel_fastfood.shtml (accessed June 23, 2008).